Marabel Morgan's
Handbook for Kitchen Survival

The Total Woman Cookbook

Also by Marabel Morgan

THE TOTAL WOMAN
TOTAL JOY
THE TOTAL WOMAN COOKBOOK

Marabel Morgan's
Handbook for Kitchen Survival

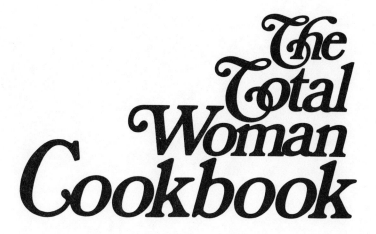

The Total Woman Cookbook

Fleming H. Revell Company
Old Tappan, New Jersey

Illustrations in *The Total Woman Cookbook*
by Russell Willeman

Library of Congress Cataloging in Publication Data

Morgan, Marabel.
    The total woman cookbook.

Includes index.
    1. Cookery. I. Title.
TX715.M844   641.5   79-26875
ISBN 0-8007-1094-0

Contents

Acknowledgments

It has been lots of fun working on this cookbook. For every winner included in this book, our family has tested, tasted, and canned an awful lot of losers.

Thanks, Charlie, Laura, and Michelle—not just for when we tested six different hot-fudge recipes (that was the fun part), but for hanging in there for the restewed tomatoes, lettuce soufflé, and the other dishes that curled your hair (and mine!).

Thanks, also, to my special friends who sent in so many recipes of all kinds. Acknowledgment is made to all whom I can recall: Florence Raber, Karen Henegar, Verna Franklin, Patsy Rooney, Kathy Jackson, Mary Wilging, Pam Wilging, Monica Rich, Peggy Wing, Sandy Buell, Dorothy Sharpe, Scarlett Zachar, Rosalyn Danner, Roz Leitman, Cindy Weinlaeder, Karol Fagaros Short, Joanne Perks, Jeanne Wolf, Jeanne Barr, Donna Jean Barr, Gail Brenner, Dorothy King, Kay Brigham, Susan Woodruff, Merrily Kimbrough, Jan Naramore, Nancy Rader, Ruth Bonham, Peggy Melitio, Alice Twigg, Jordan Davidson, Margaret Race, Gina Race, Charlyne Meyer, Martha Kettler, Delia Weinreich, Lillian Ditmer, Andrea Magoon, Brenda Drewes, Anna Brown, Barbara Miles, Don Bleau, Jan Retzke, Anita Green, Sally Mettler, Ryna and Edie of Shangri-la Spa, Sita Abrams, Mundek Schreiber, Joyce Davidson, Linda George, La Verne Airhart, Molly Ruskin, Josephine Church, and Diane Kaplus.

Introduction

How do you come down off a honeymoon?

I mean, a glorious, three-day, sleep-late, sun-and-fun, goose-bumps-and-all, room-service-knowing-looks honeymoon. The marriage books never seem to cover the day after the honeymoon.

Charlie and I returned to reality the afternoon of the fourth day. As I stepped inside our tiny apartment, I felt like an astronaut touching down on an unknown world. I would conquer this new domain, and *especially* my freshly painted, periwinkle-blue kitchen. Since I was starved, I immediately began the "conquest."

I remember shaping the ground meat into patties and asking myself for the first time, *What if Charlie doesn't like hamburgers and chocolate chip cookies every night? I could be in thick soup, already.*

I knew I had married a man whose mother was known as a super cook (one of those!), and I wondered if my cooking could ever measure up to hers. Married only ninety-six hours, and already I had begun to feel intimidated.

And then another fear struck me. What if my new, bright-eyed, and very hungry husband preferred some tastes that were beyond my expertise of culinary skills?

A few moments later Charlie headed for the kitchen. He attacked me and the hamburgers almost simultaneously. At that point, I'm sure he wouldn't have known or cared much what he ate. I put those nagging questions about menus out of my mind, and we enjoyed "playing house." I loved it.

(As I write this, it suddenly dawns on me that my standard Monday-through-Friday menu may have been a major contributing factor in the boredom that early overtook our marriage. A man can stand almost anything but boredom.)

Anyway, we survived those first few weeks on hamburgers and love. We both lost a few pounds.

Occasionally we stopped by my in-laws to visit, but when we did, I noticed that Charlie ran to the kitchen without hardly greeting anyone. He couldn't wait to look in the refrigerator or peek in the bubbling pots on the stove.

I felt mortified. I knew his mother thought I never fed him. Charlie never ran to the pots on *my* stove. But then, there never were any pots cooking on my stove, anyway. That still didn't soothe the bruises on my ego.

I was a bit confused. When Charlie announced he was hungry, I thought the food would be inconsequential. The big shock to my romantic soul came in realizing that living on love, sexually speaking, was only a few minutes out of each day (if we were lucky). The other twenty-three-plus hours were spent in working and sleeping and surviving. A large block of that time each day, nearly three hours, was spent on food—fixing it, eating it, and cleaning it up.

I turned to the cookbooks for help. I read. I thought it would be easy, but there was so much *preparation* time involved. I never realized meals could be so time-consuming.

In the first place, even the decision on *which menu* to choose sometimes took lots of time. Then there followed the time spent—or wasted—in traipsing to the store for the ingredients, figuring out the recipe, and stirring the concoction together. It was exhausting for an inexperienced bride. I was exhausted most of the time.

Two major events coincided about fourteen months after our wedding day. Our dear baby girl, Laura, was born, and Charlie was accepted at NYU's graduate law school.

On the way to New York, I acknowledged to Charlie that we were in a dining rut. I knew there was great room for improvement, so I determined to make our mealtime more appealing. I decided to try a new menu every night during our year there.

I really couldn't believe I was suggesting this. I knew it would involve hours of sorting through recipes, testing, and experimenting. But Charlie thought it was a great idea (he was far hungrier than I had realized), and my project was launched.

In the days that followed, Charlie hit the books, while Laura and I hit the streets in search of ingredients. Up and down the cobblestone streets of Greenwich Village, I pushed Laura in her buggy, as we sniffed out all sorts of curious items. In those intriguing outdoor markets, I found cheeses I had never before seen or smelled. I bought new-found fruits I hadn't known existed. Dinner each evening was an adventure in exotica.

Our tiny kitchen resembled a broom closet, and the minirefrigerator held only enough food for one day. So, combing the nooks and crannies for goodies became our morning routine. Then in the afternoon while Laura slept, I tried to transform my groceries into gastronomic masterpieces.

Some were. Some weren't. But I learned.

In my excursions through many kinds of recipes, I was surprised at some of my findings. For one thing, I discovered that Charlie seemed threatened by certain foods. He was suspicious of my casseroles, thinking I had sneaked in some wheat germ or "good-for-you" vegetables that he wouldn't like.

This discovery annoyed me, until I happened to read a survey, years later, taken among U.S. servicemen. The military polled its active members of the Army, Navy, Air Force, and Marine Corps to determine their favorite and least favorite foods.

Here are their findings:

Fifteen Best-Liked Foods

1. Milk
2. Grilled steak
3. Eggs to order
4. Corn on the cob
5. Orange juice
6. Strawberry shortcake
7. French-fried potatoes
8. Fried chicken
9. Ice cream
10. Milk shakes
11. Bacon
12. Spaghetti with meat sauce
13. Spaghetti with meatballs
14. Beer
15. Bacon-lettuce-tomato sandwich

Fifteen Least-Liked Foods

1. Carrot-raisin-celery salad
2. Canned figs
3. Boiled pigs' feet
4. Baked yellow squash
5. Kidney-bean salad

6. Creamed onions
7. French-fried cauliflower
8. Stewed prunes
9. Prune juice
10. French-fried carrots
11. Mashed rutabaga
12. Low-calorie soda
13. Fried parsnips
14. Skimmed milk
15. Buttermilk

When I showed the lists to Charlie, he agreed with many items, but then added some of his special dislikes, such as Waldorf salad, artichokes, salads with marshmallows, and "any Jell-O you can't see through."

I understood then that he wasn't just being choosy or obstinate; he was simply reflecting his personal tastes. For years I tried to change Charlie's fussy eating habits. I cooked what I knew he wouldn't eat, then cried when he wouldn't eat it. I finally gave up the crusade for lack of interest.

Today, as a mother of two teenagers (one for real and one "would-be"), I want my dishes to be marvelous, not just passable. I ask my family to rate certain meals on a scale of 1 to 10. I figure, why waste my energy on a lovely creation if no one eats it?

One night recently, Michelle, who is such a kind little soul and wouldn't hurt a flea, proposed that we take two votes—one on how well I *prepared* the dish (*my* effort), and the second vote on how well they *liked* it (*their* personal like or dislike). I appreciate the double vote. That way, I can save face.

Sometimes, the first vote doesn't even rate a 2, like that time when I went next door and forgot the pizza in the oven. When I returned to the smoke-filled house, Charlie had just nosed out the fire department in a photo finish and turned off the oven. He took the charred, stiff remains and hung them in effigy from the window on a string. That got a *minus* 3.

Having each member of the family casting his vote makes for lively discussion at the dinner table. When I ask for their scores, I feel like a platform diver in competition, waiting for the judges to hold up their fingers as I break the water.

That's my family. Keen judges. Stuffed zucchini—5, 4, 5. Ham loaf—4, 3, 3. And for an occasional winner, like chocolate soufflé—10, 10, 10.

In this book I have put together all of my 10s.

Confessions of a Chocoholic

I have a confession to make. I'm a dessert freak. In this enlightened age, when everyone knows that sugar is poison, I have this desperate, passionate craving for desserts. All day long I dream of desserts, delicacies of all kinds. In restaurants, I read the menu backwards. I order my dessert first. Succulent strawberry cheesecake, spicy apple pie, chocolate mousse. You name it, I'll eat it.

Especially chocolate. Chocolate anything. I am a "chocoholic." An avowed, died-in-the-wool, hard-core, over-the-hill, long-term, no-turning-back chocoholic. I wear a bracelet on my wrist which reads, "I'm a chocoholic. In case of emergency, feed me."

Now allow me to confess my second greatest problem in life—my weight. I gain weight faster than any woman alive. It's just not fair. When I go on a diet, I *gain* five pounds! No wonder I don't trust scales.

But for some unknown reason, food doesn't affect my family that way. I just can't understand how they can eat all the time and stay so slim. I fix the food, do all the work, don't eat that much (Oh, not *that* much!), but for me the pounds keep creeping on.

Once I attended a weight-reducing class to help lose ten unwanted pounds. The instructor told me, "Think of that weight as forty quarters of butter strung end-to-end hanging from your nose."

Forty quarters of butter?, I thought. *That's a lot of butter, Mac. Or, to be more brutal, that's a lot of fat I'm dragging around every day.*

When I returned home that day, I took a ruler and measured a butter stick just for kicks. Then I multiplied that by forty quarters. To my surprise the line of butter I was dragging from my nose was sixteen-feet long!

I tried to imagine the practical problems of living with a sixteen-foot nose—problems like revolving doors and hot burners and our puppy, Total, who nips at every moving object.

That night I had a horrible nightmare. I dreamed my nose truly was sixteen-feet long. After hours of tossing restlessly, I told myself,

Enough of this nonsense. I crawled out of bed and headed for the bathroom.

There in the full and sudden light I stood half asleep before the mirror. The shock was almost too much to bear, but I was never so relieved to see that my nose was back to normal. In fact, it was the only *safe* part of me. Then I turned around and found where those forty quarters of butter were hanging.

I still think of my sixteen-foot nose, occasionally. Especially after a big weekend, when it stretches and contracts unbelievably.

To eat or not to eat, that is always the question. The everyday question that I must face, along with my family's everyday question, *"When* do we eat?"

Cannelloni on Review

What mother hasn't spent all afternoon in a hot kitchen preparing a gourmet spinach soufflé, only to hear Fred and Junior announce in unison, "Oh, yuk! What's that? I don't want any."

In the preparation of this book, I have cooked all kinds of new and sometimes strange dishes, and the reactions from my family have been predictably varied.

I must confess another problem of mine. I don't mind an honest evaluation, but I am always amazed when people make an instant analysis about a dish they haven't even tasted before.

I remember the first time it happened at our house. I was beginning to experiment with new foods, and I casually mentioned at breakfast that we'd have cannelloni for dinner that evening. My girls had never tried that dish before, so I thought it best to warn them. (*Better now than at the dinner table,* I thought).

This time Michelle was the first to react, almost as though she had been waiting to press her buzzer in "Name That Tune."

"Oh, *yuk!* " she said with the same disdain she reserves for Worms Tetrazzini.

"Oh, yuk?", asked Charlie. "Why do you say that? Have you ever tasted cannelloni?"

I thought to myself, *Wonder of wonders, another county heard from.* With Charlie coming to my rescue, there were three-fourths of the votes in. It was neck and neck, two to one.

"No," she said, "but I just know I don't like it. Don't ask me why."

I could see Charlie was a bit irritated. He went back to questioning his witness. "That's impossible, honey. There must be some reason why."

"Well," she said thoughtfully, "it's just too spicy for my tender little taste buds."

We all laughed. I mean, how do you handle that one?

Charlie tried. "Michelle," he started, "Any new food deserves at least *one* chance. If you don't give it that one chance, it's not fair." (*Playing on her concept of fairness! To Michelle, everything in life is either fair or not fair.*)

"I'll tell you what," he explained. "Tell your little brain to tell your little taste buds, 'Hey, I think I'm going to like this stuff.' Then watch what happens. Pretty soon your little sniffer will say, 'Not bad, a bit of cheese, hmmmmmm . . .' Then your little taste buds will see this new-fangled stuff coming inside and say, 'I *like* it.' Up goes the message to your brain, 'I like it.'

"And then, later on, you'll say, 'By the way, Mom, what was that great stuff we had for dinner last week? You know, that cheesy stuff? Oh, yeah, cannelloni. When are we going to have that again?' "

That ended our discussion of cannelloni. After the meal, Michelle left the table still unconvinced. But I must add a postscript to the story.

Three months later I made the same dish again, and this time Michelle tried it and ate it. Charlie winked at me when she reached for seconds.

Another Italian "aficionada" was born.

The First-Bite Rule

Did you know that a dog is presumed legally tame until he has taken his first bite? If it's any consolation, I didn't either, until my lawyer-husband told me after Total had nipped the mailman.

Regardless of the size of the dog and his teeth, unless he has bitten someone else before, in some states he is presumed harmless. That means, if he chooses you for his very first bite, you can't sue the owner. Some comfort!

You might remember that little point of law the next time you visit a neighbor and are met at the door by a panting, hairy monster (her dog, not her husband!) greeting you at eye level.

As a result of The Great Cannelloni Episode, Charlie and I installed "The First-Bite Rule" at our house. That means any new dish is presumed harmless until each one of the family takes the first bite. Only after that can it be considered dangerous.

While I'm not in the business to force my family to eat Waldorf salad with liverloaf, I feel anyone can survive one bite. If they don't take at least one bite, how will they ever know whether they like it or not?

Not long ago, Michelle was afraid to try creamed spinach for the first time. "I hate it," she protested.

We reminded her of "The First-Bite Rule," and then listened to "Ten Good Reasons Why the Rule Should Be Abolished for an Eight-Year-Old." Finally she took the first bite, grimaced, and quivered, before quickly swallowing some milk to wash it down.

"OK," I said. "How was it?"

"Well," she drawled, "I don't hate it, but I don't *love* it either."

That's all I could ever ask. At least she tasted it. Beyond that, it's up to her personal taste and preference.

But if she ever ends up marrying a farmer, I'll bet they'll never grow spinach.

Caveman Stew

The menus in this book are our family favorites and bring cheers at our dining table. To help save time, I have arranged the menus according to the occasion.

As an example, if Fred left home mad this morning, tonight you might try "Time to Reconcile." On the other hand, if Fred had one of those days at the office and you've farmed out the kids for tonight, slip into something comfortable with "Time for Romance."

If Fred's in the TV room watching the game, turn to "For Men Only." If it's been Dullsville for weeks, let the kids help with "Just for Fun" or "Ho-Hum Tuesdays."

Psychologist Clyde Narramore says that people are often down on what they're not up on. I believe that's especially true about cooking. As a new bride, when I tried to plan an entire week of menus in advance, I always bogged down on the first day. A few years later with two little ankle-biters tagging at my heels, I didn't have the energy, let alone time, to plan magnificent meals.

I love the cartoon of a caveman and cavewoman sitting around the campfire with a pot bubbling while Mrs. Cavewoman drolls, "Sometimes I wish you'd never invented fire. I hate to cook."

So many women have told me the same thing. Cooking can be a real pain in the neck. After years of too many disasters, much mediocrity, and some blazing successes, I have found some menus that work for me.

This is not an all-inclusive cookbook, so don't look for exotic French-fried squid and grasshopper mousse. I have purposely not included some very exotic recipes or ones that take three days to prepare. Who has time to start dinner last Tuesday? These meals are delicious, nutritious, and easy on the cook.

For those of you who are just starting out, I am eager to share what I've learned. Maybe you can eliminate some of the mistakes I've made. Of course, if you've already got it all together, you don't need me. Marvelous cooks won't require this book; they can write their own. In fact, I recommend it.

Yet, regardless of your cooking skills, let me suggest a super project to work on each day. Arrange your notebook on the counter while you're cooking dinner and compile your *own* cookbook by personalizing your recipes. At least you won't need to search again through endless piles for that special recipe. And you'll feel so satisfied when your losers are weeded out, and your drawers are clean.

My original goal was not to publish this book, but to simplify my life, with all my favorite recipes in one notebook. As Charlie says, "Even if no one else is interested, it doesn't matter. At least we're eating better."

I believe that creating in the kitchen is just as an authentic form of self-expression as art or music or science. My kitchen is no longer a new world to be conquered, it's my favorite room: my laboratory where I experiment; my studio where I create. I believe I'm building healthy bodies and happy memories. I am refueling not only tummies, but also hearts.

Like to join me? OK, let's start at the very beginning. Desserts!

1
Just Desserts

Cakes Royale
The Cookie Mother
Pies and Other Assorted Vices

Cakes Royale

MY FAVORITE CHOCOLATE CAKE
Serves 16

1 cup unsifted, unsweetened cocoa	½ teaspoon baking powder
2 cups boiling water	1 cup butter
2¾ cups sifted flour	2½ cups sugar
2 teaspoons baking soda	1 teaspoon instant coffee powder
½ teaspoon salt	4 eggs
	1 tablespoon vanilla

1. Preheat oven to 350°. In small mixing bowl, mix cocoa and boiling water with wire whisk until smooth. Set aside to cool. Sift flour with soda, salt, and baking powder and set aside. Grease and lightly flour three 9-inch round cake pans.

2. In large bowl, beat at high speed, butter, sugar, instant coffee, eggs, and vanilla until light—about 5 minutes. Stir in flour mixture (in fourths), alternately with cocoa mixture (in thirds), beginning and ending with flour mixture. Do not overbeat.

3. Divide evenly into pans; smooth top. Bake 20 to 25 minutes, or until surface springs back when gently pressed with fingertip. Cool in pans 10 minutes. Carefully loosen sides with spatula; remove from pans; cool on racks.

TIP: I often frost two layers and freeze one layer to use later. One secret to any good cake is having all ingredients at room temperature.

FUDGE FROSTING
Makes enough for three 9-inch layers

3 cups sugar	Dash of salt
1 cup milk	3 tablespoons light corn syrup
4 squares unsweetened chocolate	⅓ cup butter
	2 teaspoons vanilla

1. In 3-quart saucepan over medium heat, bring to boil sugar, milk, chocolate, salt, and corn syrup, stirring until sugar dissolves. Reduce heat to medium and cook, stirring occasionally, until syrup reaches soft-ball stage (234° on candy thermometer).

2. Remove from heat. Add butter and vanilla but do not stir. Cool at room temperature (without stirring) to 110° or until bottom of pan feels just warm, about 1 hour.

3. Turn out into small bowl of mixer and beat at high speed until frosting is creamy and begins to hold its shape. I divide the cooked frosting into *two* bowls because it sets up faster. I beat one bowl, frost layers, beat next bowl, and finish cake. If frosting becomes too stiff, beat in a little warm milk or hot water, about a spoonful.

4. When frosting is just about ready, I beat with a spoon instead of electric mixer, so I can spread it immediately. Frosting spreads easily and maintains gloss if spatula is dipped in hot water.

For two 9-inch layers, use:

2 cups sugar	Dash of salt
¾ cup milk	2 tablespoons corn syrup
2 squares unsweetened chocolate	¼ cup butter
	1 teaspoon vanilla

COCOA CAKE WITH COCOA CRUNCH FROSTING
Serves 12

2 cups flour
2 cups sugar
½ teaspoon salt
½ cup butter
½ cup shortening
⅓ cup unsweetened cocoa

2 eggs, slightly beaten
½ cup buttermilk
1 teaspoon baking soda
¼ teaspoon cinnamon
3 teaspoons vanilla extract

1. Preheat oven to 350°. In large bowl, sift flour with sugar and salt; set aside. Grease a 13 x 9 x 2-inch baking pan.

2. In small saucepan, combine butter, shortening, cocoa, and 1 cup water; bring to boil. Pour over flour mixture. Mix well.

3. Add eggs, buttermilk, soda, cinnamon, and vanilla; beat just until smooth. Immediately pour into prepared pan.

4. Bake 40 to 45 minutes, or until surface springs back when gently pressed with fingertip.

COCOA CRUNCH FROSTING

½ cup butter
¼ cup unsweetened cocoa
6 tablespoons milk
1 pound powdered sugar

1 teaspoon vanilla
½ cup grated coconut
1 cup chopped nuts

1. In medium saucepan, mix butter, cocoa, and milk; bring just to boiling. Remove from heat.

2. Add sugar and vanilla; beat until smooth. Stir in coconut and nuts. Spread over hot cake. Cool in pan on wire rack.

BROWN SUGAR POUND CAKE
Serves 18–20
This cake freezes beautifully.

3 sticks (¾ pound) butter
1 8-ounce package cream
   cheese, softened
2 cups sugar
1 cup light brown sugar
6 eggs

1 tablespoon vanilla
2 teaspoons baking powder
3 cups flour
½ teaspoon salt
¼ teaspoon mace (optional)

1. Preheat oven to 325°. In large mixing bowl, cream together butter and cream cheese, beating in sugars with electric mixer. Add eggs one at a time and continue to beat. Add vanilla.

2. Sift baking powder and flour and stir ⅓ at a time into butter mixture. With spoon, blend until smooth but do not overbeat.

3. Pour batter into greased and floured 10-inch tube pan or two 7¾-inch tube pans. Bake for 1 hour and 20 minutes for 10-inch pan, or 1 hour for smaller cakes, or until cake tests done. Cool in pan 10 minutes. Turn out on rack and cool completely. Dust with powdered sugar, or use either of glazes below.

SUGAR GLAZE

2 tablespoons butter
1 cup sugar

½ cup water
1 teaspoon vanilla

Combine above ingredients and bring to a boil. While cake is warm, remove from pan and slowly add glaze with pastry brush. (It takes about 20 minutes to glaze the cake, but it's worth it.)

APRICOT GLAZE

1 cup apricot jam

1 cup sugar

Put jam through sieve. Bring jam and sugar to boil. Simmer until mixture coats spoon. Spread on cake with pastry brush.

FRENCH ORANGE NUT CAKE
I love to make this luscious cake in small loaf pans and freeze ahead for Christmas gifts.

2 sticks butter
2 cups sugar
4 cups flour
4 eggs
1½ cups buttermilk
1 teaspoon salt

1½ teaspoons baking soda
2 tablespoons grated orange rind
1 cup dates (or raisins) chopped fine
1 cup pecans or walnuts, chopped

1. Preheat oven to 325°. Cream butter and sugar. Beat in 1 egg at a time. Add flour and salt alternately with 1 cup buttermilk.

2. Add soda to ½ cup buttermilk and add to mixture, then stir in dates, nuts, and orange rind. Bake in well-buttered 10-inch tube pan for 70 minutes or until cake tests done. If using small loaf pans, 7½ x 3½ x 2-inch, bake 45 minutes. Test for doneness.

SAUCE

1 to 2 cups sugar

2 cups fresh orange juice

Heat sugar and orange juice until sugar is completely dissolved. When cake is done, let stand for 10 minutes; then spoon sauce over hot cake until all is used. It takes a little while to soak in. Let cake sit in pan overnight. In morning, remove to covered cake container.

SOUR CREAM WALNUT CAKE
Scrumptious!

1 cup butter
2⅞ cups sugar
6 eggs separated
2 teaspoons vanilla extract
3 cups cake flour, sifted

¼ teaspoon baking soda
½ teaspoon salt
1 cup sour cream
1 cup walnuts, finely chopped
Powdered sugar

1. Preheat oven to 350°. Cream butter and sugar together. Add egg yolks one at a time and beat well after each addition. Add vanilla and set aside.

2. Sift cake flour and soda together. Set aside.

3. Beat egg whites with salt until stiff peaks form.

4. Stir flour mixture into egg mixture alternately with sour cream. Sprinkle nuts on top and fold into batter. Fold beaten egg whites into batter. Pour into greased and floured 10-inch tube pan and bake 1 to 1¼ hours or until done. Cool cake in pan, on a rack. When cool, turn out of pan and dust with powdered sugar.

VARIATION: If you omit the nuts, you have a delicious pound cake.

OATMEAL CAKE WITH COCONUT TOPPING

1 cup Quick Quaker Oats	2 eggs
1¼ cups boiling water	1½ cups flour
½ cup butter	1 teaspoon baking soda
1 cup sugar	1 teaspoon cinnamon
1 cup brown sugar	½ teaspoon salt
2 teaspoons vanilla	¼ teaspoon nutmeg

1. Preheat oven to 350°. Grease and flour 9-inch square pan. Pour boiling water over oats. Let stand for 20 minutes.

2. Beat butter and sugars until smooth. Add eggs one at a time, beating until mixed. Stir in vanilla and oats.

3. Sift dry ingredients together and stir into mixture. Pour into prepared pan and bake 55 minutes or until done.

TOPPING

½ stick butter, melted	½ cup chopped nuts
½ cup brown sugar	½ cup coconut
3 tablespoons light cream or evaporated milk	

Mix ingredients together and bring to a boil, stirring constantly, for 2 minutes. Spread on hot cake and brown under broiler until topping is bubbly.

The Cookie Mother

Chocolate Dream Bars
Walnut Dream Bars
Double-Layered Cookies
Luscious Apricot Squares
Raspberry Thumbprint Cookies
Date-Nut Cookies
Shortbread

Please check the Index for other cookie recipes which appear with complete menus.

CHOCOLATE DREAM BARS
Makes 24

BOTTOM LAYER

1 cup flour   ½ cup butter
3 tablespoons brown sugar

1. Preheat oven to 350°. Mix flour and brown sugar together. Work in butter with pastry cutter or two knives until mixture has a pie-crust consistency.

2. Pat mixture in bottom of buttered 13 x 9-inch baking pan, and bake about 10 minutes or until brown. While crust is baking, prepare top layer. (You may use a 9-inch square pan for a thicker cookie, but increase baking time 5 minutes for each layer.)

TOP LAYER

1 cup brown sugar   ¼ teaspoon salt
2 tablespoons flour   6 ounces of semisweet chocolate
2 eggs   chips
½ teaspoon baking powder   ½ teaspoon instant coffee
1½ teaspoons vanilla

1. Blend brown sugar, flour, and baking powder together. Beat eggs and blend into sugar mixture. Stir in vanilla, salt, coffee, and chocolate chips.

2. Pour and spread mixture evenly over baked crust in pan, and bake for 20 minutes more, or until brown.

3. When cool, cut into bars and sprinkle with powdered sugar.

VARIATION: For WALNUT DREAM BARS, omit chocolate chips in top layer, increase sugar to 1½ cups, and mix in 1 cup broken English walnuts.

DOUBLE-LAYERED COOKIES

⅔ cup butter or shortening
   (or mixture of both)
½ cup sugar
½ cup brown sugar
2 egg yolks
1 tablespoon water
1 teaspoon vanilla
2 cups flour

1 teaspoon baking powder
½ teaspoon salt
1 6-ounce package semisweet
   chocolate chips
2 egg whites
¼ teaspoon cream of tartar
1 cup brown sugar

1. Preheat oven to 350°. Cream butter and sugars. Beat in yolks, water, and vanilla.

2. Mix flour, baking powder, and salt together and stir into butter mixture. Pat into 13 x 9-inch pan. Sprinkle evenly with chocolate chips.

3. Beat egg whites and cream of tartar until stiff. Beat in 1 cup brown sugar. Spoon over cookie mixture in pan, spreading evenly into corners. Bake for 30 minutes. Cut into squares while warm.

LUSCIOUS APRICOT SQUARES
Makes 16

1 cup dried apricots
½ cup water
1 slice lemon
½ cup butter, softened
¼ cup sugar
1⅓ cups sifted flour
½ teaspoon baking powder
¼ teaspoon salt

1¼ cups packed light or dark
   brown sugar
2 eggs
⅔ cup chopped walnuts
½ cup chopped coconut
   (optional)
1 teaspoon vanilla
Powdered sugar

1. Preheat oven to 350°. Mix apricots, water, and lemon in small saucepan. Bring mixture to a boil; reduce heat, cover, and simmer for 30 minutes. Stir in sugar and cook 1 minute. Remove lemon slice. Put mixture in blender to make puree. Set aside to cool.

2. In large bowl, cream butter and ¼ cup sugar; stir in 1 cup flour until crumbly; pack ½ of mixture into greased 9 x 9-inch cake pan firmly and evenly with fingertips. Cover with waxed paper, pressing with palm to make smooth, compact layer. Remove paper. Bake 20 minutes or until lightly browned.

3. Mix together ⅓ cup flour, baking powder, and salt. In large bowl, with electric mixer at medium speed, beat brown sugar and eggs. Stir in flour mixture, walnuts, vanilla, coconut, and apricot mixture. Spread over baked layer and bake 25 to 30 minutes more until golden. Cool on rack in pan about 15 minutes. Cut in squares. Dip in powdered sugar. Store in airtight container.

RASPBERRY THUMBPRINT COOKIES
Makes 3 dozen

1 cup (2 sticks) unsalted butter	**2 egg yolks**
½ cup sugar	**2 egg whites**
2 cups flour	**2 cups chopped nuts**
½ teaspoon salt	**½ cup red raspberry preserves**

1. Cream butter and sugar. Add flour, salt, and egg yolks and beat 1 minute. Chill.

2. Shape into 1-inch balls. Dip balls into slightly beaten egg white, then roll in chopped nuts. Place 1½ inches apart on greased cookie sheet, allowing room for spreading.

3. Preheat oven to 375°. Flatten cookies slightly, and indent centers with thumb or thimble. Fill with preserves. Bake for 10 to 12 minutes or until lightly browned. Store in tightly covered cookie tin with waxed paper between layers.

DATE-NUT COOKIES
Makes 4 dozen

½ cup butter
¾ cup sugar
1 8-ounce package dates,
    chopped

2½ cups Rice Krispies cereal
1 cup chopped pecans
Powdered sugar

Mix butter, sugar, and dates in saucepan. Bring to boil; cook, stirring constantly, 3 minutes. Remove from stove. Stir in cereal and pecans. Roll in balls; then roll in powdered sugar.

SHORTBREAD COOKIES
Makes 16

⅔ cup sweet butter, at room
    temperature
¼ teaspoon salt (omit if using
    salted butter)

½ cup powdered sugar
1½ cups plus 2 tablespoons
    sifted flour
Apricot preserves (optional)

1. Preheat oven to 325°. Sift flour, sugar, and salt into butter and mix into ball with hands. Press mixture into 9-inch quiche pan with loose bottom. Prick surface all over with fork and mark into 16 wedges, cutting with knife halfway through dough.

2. Bake until firm when pressed gently in center, or about 40 to 50 minutes. Cut into wedges while hot. Cookies should be lightly golden, not brown.

VARIATIONS: 1. Roll dough into 1-inch balls and press down lightly with bottom of glass. Bake for 20 minutes or until very lightly browned. For an elegant touch, moisten back of almond with water and lay on top of each baked cookie. Dust with powdered sugar, if desired.

2. Roll dough into 1-inch balls and make thumbprint indentation in each ball. Fill with tiny dab of apricot preserves. Bake until just barely golden, about 20 minutes.

Pies and Other Assorted Vices

If I told you my very favorite pie of all time, I'd have to say it is Peaches 'n Cream. Or maybe Blackberry or, umm, Red Raspberry. And I just remembered, Concord Grape. Oh, what an experience! Makes my taste buds tingle just to think of it. Better just say fruit pie.

I made my first pie when I was eight years old. I still remember that day. My mother was sick in bed, so I had free reign of the kitchen. My first creation was a raisin pie with a buttery crust. I used all butter for the shortening, not knowing that was quite extravagant and really not desirable. But the pie was a big hit, and I was hooked on baking.

I still love to bake pies. I'd like to open a pie stand for husbands where they could stop on their way home from work and pick up a present that all would enjoy. But better than that, here are the recipes. Create your own (or teach your children to do it), and save me the time to make my own.

PIE PASTRY

So many people are afraid of pie crust. The secret is in step 2 below. When pastry cleans the side of the bowl and makes itself into a ball, it's ready. That's all there is to it. But if you don't have the time, buy prepared shells.

Makes two 9-inch pie shells (topless) or 1 pie with top crust.

2 cups flour, chilled   **1 tablespoon chilled butter**
1 teaspoon salt   **4–5 tablespoons ice water, or**
⅔ cup shortening, chilled   **more if necessary**

1. Mix flour and salt. Cut in half of shortening with a pastry cutter (or two knives) until mixture looks like cornmeal. Cut in remaining shortening and butter until mixture looks like small peas.

2. Sprinkle ice water over mixture a spoonful at a time, stirring lightly with fork until dough begins to hold together. Add water gradually until mixture pulls together into ball and cleans sides of bowl.

3. Shape into 2 balls. Wrap in wax paper and refrigerate for 1 hour. Roll out on floured tea towel. Fit into pie pans. For pies that require a baked shell, prick all over with fork. Bake at 475° for 8 minutes. For pies that require an unbaked pastry, refrigerate shell until ready to fill.

GRAHAM-CRACKER CRUST
Makes one 9-inch crust

1⅓ cups crushed graham   **¼ cup melted butter**
crackers   **¼ cup chopped nuts (optional)**
⅓ cup sugar   **Dash of cinnamon (optional)**

Mix all ingredients together. Pat mixture on bottom and sides of lightly buttered 9-inch pie plate. Bake 8 minutes in 375° oven.

NUT CRUST

1 cup finely chopped nuts ¼ cup sugar
(pecans, walnuts, almonds, 4 tablespoons butter at room
or Brazil nuts) temperature

Mix ingredients together. Press onto bottom and sides of lightly buttered 9-inch pie plate. Bake 6–8 minutes in 400° oven. Cool.

OPEN-FACED HEAVENLY PEACH PIE
Serves 8

1 9-inch unbaked pie crust 4 tablespoons flour
½ cup broken pecans (optional) ¼ teaspoon salt
6 fresh peaches, peeled and cut ¼ teaspoon nutmeg
in half ½ teaspoon cinnamon
½ cup white sugar 1 cup coffee cream or heavy
½ cup brown sugar cream

Preheat oven to 400°. Sprinkle pecans on bottom of unbaked pie crust. Put peach halves, cut side up in unbaked pie crust. Mix rest of ingredients together and pour over peaches. Bake 45 minutes or until crust is golden brown. Serve warm or cold.

VARIATION: Substitute 5 cups of raspberries, blackberries, or blueberries in place of peaches. Each taste is just sublime.

KEY LIME PIE
Serves 8

Just after the Civil War, in the devastated South, one of the few foods available was sweetened condensed milk, a new product developed in 1858. Cooks squeezed limes grown in the Florida Keys into the condensed milk to complement the milk's sweetness, and accidentally hit upon a mixture firm enough to be a pie filling.

3 eggs, yolks and whites separated
1 14-ounce can sweetened condensed milk
½ cup lime or lemon juice
Few drops of green food coloring (optional)

1 teaspoon grated lime peel
1 9-inch baked and cooled pastry shell or graham-cracker crust shell
1 cup sweetened whipped cream

1. In medium-sized bowl with electric mixer, beat 3 yolks and 1 egg white until thick and light-colored. Beat in condensed milk, lime juice, and grated lime. Add food coloring if you wish. (In its natural state, Key Lime Pie filling is pale yellow.)

2. Pour mixture into prepared pie shell. Chill about 6 hours. When ready to serve, spread sweetened whipped cream over filling and garnish with twisted lime slice. This pie also freezes beautifully.

OLD-FASHIONED APPLE PIE WITH FRENCH CRUMB TOPPING
Serves 8

7 cups sliced, peeled MacIntosh or good cooking apples (about 7)
½ cup packed light brown sugar
½ teaspoon nutmeg
Dash of ground cloves
1 tablespoon lemon juice or 1½ teaspoons grated lemon rind

½ teaspoon cinnamon
1 tablespoon cornstarch or flour
4 vanilla wafers, crushed, or 3 tablespoons finely ground nuts (optional)
1 9-inch unbaked pastry shell

FRENCH CRUMB TOPPING

⅓ cup butter
⅓ cup brown sugar

¾ cup flour
½ cup chopped nuts (optional)

1. Preheat oven to 425°. In large bowl, combine sugar and cornstarch (or flour). Mix together with apples, brown sugar, spices, and lemon juice.

2. Sprinkle wafers or nuts on bottom of pie shell. (This keeps crust from becoming soggy.) Spoon apple mixture into pie shell.

3. Make French Crumb Topping by mixing ⅓ cup butter and ⅓ cup brown sugar together. Cut in ¾ cup flour. Stir in nuts. Sprinkle topping over apples in pie plate. Bake for 50 minutes or until topping is golden and apples are tender.

NOTE: If you prefer to use conventional top crust, brush unbaked top crust with egg yolk and 1 tablespoon cream mixed together. Dust with sifted powdered sugar when pie comes out of oven. Or use the following topping on top of the crust before baking.

2 tablespoons flour	**3 tablespoons dark corn syrup**
¼ cup brown sugar	**2 tablespoons butter, softened**
¼ cup chopped nuts	

Mix all ingredients together and spread over unbaked top crust. Bake for about 50 minutes.

TIP: For a lovely taste thrill, mix 3 or 4 teaspoons of cinnamon into 1 quart softened vanilla ice cream. Refreeze. Serve a scoop of the cinnamon ice cream on warm apple-pie slices.

CONCORD GRAPE PIE
Serves 8
Out of this world!

1 pastry for 2-crust, 9-inch pie	**1 tablespoon grated orange rind**
5½ cups Concord grapes	**(optional)**
1½ cups sugar	**Dash of salt**
4½ tablespoons flour	**1½ tablespoons butter**
1½ teaspoons lemon juice	**1 quart vanilla ice cream**
	(optional)

1. Preheat oven to 425°. Slip pulp out of skins and set skins aside.

2. Put pulp in saucepan with no water and bring to rolling boil. While hot, rub pulp through strainer into mixing bowl to remove seeds. Combine strained pulp and skins.

3. Mix sugar and flour; add with lemon juice, rind, and salt to grape mixture. Build up pastry slightly around edge of pie to pre-

vent juices from running over. Pour grape mixture into pastry-lined pie pan. Dot with butter.

4. Cover with top crust or lattice of pastry. Bake 40–45 minutes. Cool. Add scoop of vanilla ice cream on top of each slice.

PECAN CHESS PIE
Serves 8

1 unbaked 9-inch pastry shell   **3 eggs**
1 cup light brown sugar   **4 tablespoons buttermilk**
½ cup sugar   **1 teaspoon vanilla extract**
1 tablespoon flour   **1 cup coarsely chopped pecans**
½ cup butter, melted   **Whipped cream (optional)**

1. Preheat oven to 325°. In a medium-sized bowl mix sugars and flour. Add the melted butter and mix with a wire whisk or fork.

2. Add eggs one at a time, beating well; add milk and vanilla and mix well.

3. Pour into pastry shell. Sprinkle chopped pecans evenly over top. Bake about 45 minutes, until filling is set and crust is lightly browned. Remove pie from oven and cool on a wire rack at least two hours before cutting. Serve cold with whipped cream if desired.

RASPBERRY DREAM PIE
Serves 10
Easy as can be. Just hold the beater for 15 minutes.

1 9- or 10-inch baked pie shell   **1 tablespoon lemon juice**
2 egg whites   **½ cup whipping cream, whipped**
Dash of salt   **1 teaspoon vanilla**
¾ cup sugar
1 10-ounce package frozen rasp-
  berries, partially thawed
  and drained

1. Beat egg whites and salt until frothy. Add sugar slowly and beat until well mixed.

2. Add raspberries and lemon juice and beat at high speed for 10–15 minutes, until thick. Fold in whipped cream and vanilla.
3. Pour mixture into baked, cooled pie shell. Freeze 4 hours.

VARIATION: For RASPBERRY MOUSSE pour mixture into 2-quart mold or individual dessert dishes. Freeze 4 hours.

2
The Brunch Bunch

Sunrise Easter
Happy Holiday
Fun Raising
Florida Favorite

The Forgotten Meal Revisited

Breakfast is the one meal that most every American eats early in the morning, but can't recall what it was a half hour later.

Although the breakfast meal has some very real possibilities, the problem is that it usually happens in the morning.

Whatley wrote, "Lose an hour in the morning and you will be all day hunting for it." Around the Morgan household, we go through several rather distinct stages each morning hunting for that lost hour:

6:33 A.M.: *The "Oh, No! Not Already!" Stage.* This usually comes very early, due to a barking dog or a telephone call or that dreadful alarm clock, whichever occurs first. It matters not *who's* up first, because, within minutes, everyone is aroused by the first one to stumble around in a stupor.

7:07 A.M.: *The "Sleep-Walk Procession" Stage.* The procession starts at each bedroom, then makes a pit stop at the bathroom, winds its way through the living room, back through the dining room, and concludes at the kitchen table.

The order in line may differ, but the cast of characters is the same. Michelle usually pads in first. Laura, our teenager in her sleep shirt, is often the last to arrive, just in time to collapse on the table.

The time at which Charlie staggers in (and the mood which matches his entrance) depends on how long he's been outside looking for the paper in the bushes.

And then there's Yours Truly, in bathrobe and curlers, reaching for the utensils by braille.

7:13 A.M.: *The "Gathering of the Unconscious" Stage.* This time period is usually followed by the *"I'm Starving to Death, When Do We Eat?" Stage,* and (a) is high on smells (burnt toast, strong coffee, peanut butter, and jelly); (b) is low on conversation (in fact, no *intelligible* words—just an occasional jungle-type sound); and (c) takes about four minutes of time.

7:36 A.M.: *The "Who's in the Bathroom?" Stage.* This is always an interesting phenomenon to observe, because there's no way mathematically that four people can go into three bathrooms at once, equally and peacefully. Morgan's Law says that the one who waits for a bathroom always selects the slowest one.

7:56 A.M.: *The "Chinese Fire-Drill" Stage.* Since Charlie leaves the house at eight o'clock to drop off the girls at school, the fire drill starts at 7:56 A.M.

It is usually precipitated by the announcement of (a) lost science homework; or (b) a missing shoe that "Mom lost"; or (c) a broken shoestring; or (d) all of the above. Astonishingly, we're all wide awake within four brief minutes. At least medical science should be pleased that everyone's heart rate picks up suddenly before they drive off to face the cruel world.

8:06 A.M.: *The "Calm After the Storm" Stage.* I return to the kitchen. Pure bliss. The countertops are a mess, but the silence is golden. I begin to sing to myself, "When peace like a river. . . ."

Whoever invented breakfast anyway? I looked it up once in an encyclopedia. I was surprised to find that it all started in A.D. 931, when Bernard Breakfast, a cabinet maker from Cleveland, inherited a coffee plantation with a sizeable herd of cows, chickens, and pigs. . . .

And since I'm not even sure of my own name at that ghastly hour of the morning, how can I begin experimenting with recipes? (I fear explosions!) For me, the first planned recipes of the day are for brunch.

From Grape-Nuts to Widgets

Speaking of brunches . . . as Grape-Nuts are neither grapes nor nuts, brunch is neither breakfast nor lunch. Brunch does not fall within the traditional breakfast, lunch, and dinner sacrosanct time zones, and thus it has somehow acquired an illegitimate status in a few elite circles.

For example, Emily Post once wrote: "Do not give encouragement to that single-headed, double-bodied deformity of language, 'brunch.' The word is an ungracious one which furthermore has a hurried lunch-wagon suggestiveness. Brunch-breakfast at lunchtime calls to mind standees at a lunch counter but not the beauty of hospitable living."

To me, the very word *brunch* conjures up an informal, congenial setting, where cool breezes are stirring and my guests are totally relaxed (probably because they're still sleepy). No hurry-scurry, just a slow-moving atmosphere, like a cat stretching her paws after a nap. Controlled slow motion.

A brunch has some terrific benefits:

1. For the most part, a brunch can be prepared ahead of time, and—for me—that's good news. Regardless of whether I'm entertaining the tennis team or late-rising friends in the guest room or even my own family, I can still set it all up ahead of time. Then I'm free to put up my feet, too.

2. A brunch sounds special to children, since the food is different than usual—half breakfast, half lunch, but more elaborate than either. Still, brunch is seldom used for the kids at our house. I can usually sell eggs and cornflakes at 7:30 A.M. But after nine o'clock, I'm intruding on "the Hamburger Zone," and I could probably sell left-handed widgets faster than scrambled eggs!

3. A brunch buffet is an easy way to serve a crowd—an inexpensive yet impressive way to serve a large group of adults, teenagers, or children alike, open-house style.

4. A brunch can also accommodate many different schedules when people may be arriving at unpredictable times. And when the Christmas season is filled with parties, a holiday brunch usually doesn't compete with a lot of other brunches on the block.

5. A brunch can be as informal as you wish. Unlike many eat-and-run lunches, a brunch is usually more relaxed and informal. Instead of fixing breakfast and then lunch two hours later, I can kill two meals with one brunch. This permits me time out of the kitchen to be with my friends. They love to stay on and on and on. . . . But that's another problem. (Please turn to "Unexpected Dinner Guests" for some suggestions on how to solve it.)

Sunrise Easter

Strawberries Chantilly
Eggs in Toast Nests
Cheese Grits Soufflé
Glazed Lemon Bread
Venezuelan Flan

STRAWBERRIES CHANTILLY
Serves 8

3 pints strawberries (large, if possible)
3 tablespoons sugar

½ teaspoon lemon juice
¾ cup heavy cream
1 teaspoon vanilla

1. Wash berries gently, dry on paper towels, and remove stems. Place berries in glass serving dish. Sprinkle with 1½ tablespoons sugar and lemon juice. Sprinkle 2 tablespoons boiling water over berries and toss very gently. Refrigerate 2 hours.

2. Whip cream until stiff, with remaining 1½ tablespoons sugar and vanilla. (A spoonful of light Karo syrup folded into whipped cream keeps it stable and prevents weeping.) Serve alongside berries in pretty bowl.

EGGS IN TOAST NESTS
Serves 8
The men just love these. At our Easter breakfast, one of our guests ate six!

12 slices bread
½ cup butter, melted

12 small eggs
2 tablespoons butter

1. Trim crusts off bread slices. Brush both sides with melted butter. Fit into large buttered muffin cups or custard cups. Press down slightly with fingers so bread will fit in cup.

2. Bake in 325° oven for 15 minutes until lightly toasted. Remove from oven. (I do this step the night before and cover cups with plastic wrap.)

3. Break an egg into each toast cup. Add salt and pepper, and dot with butter. Cover lightly with foil. Bake in 350° oven 12 minutes, or until done.

4. Loosen cups with spatula and serve hot on platter with sausage links. Garnish with sprigs of parsley.

CHEESE GRITS SOUFFLÉ
Serves 8
Also called Georgia Ice Cream

1½ cups quick grits
2 teaspoons salt
6 cups boiling water
1 pound grated Cheddar
   cheese
3 eggs, beaten

Dash of Tabasco sauce
1½ sticks butter, melted
1 tablespoon seasoned salt
⅛ teaspoon paprika
1 teaspoon Worcestershire
   sauce

1. Cook grits and salt in water for 5 minutes. (If regular grits are used, cook 20 minutes.)

2. Mix all ingredients and pour into well-greased 3-quart casserole. May be refrigerated overnight. Bake 1 hour at 350° or 2½ hours at 275°.

GLAZED LEMON BREAD
Makes 2 loaves

2 cups unsifted all-purpose flour
1½ teaspoons baking powder
¼ teaspoon salt
2 teaspoons grated lemon peel
½ cup butter
1 cup sugar

2 eggs
1 teaspoon vanilla
⅓ cup milk
¾ cup chopped walnuts or
   pecans

1. Preheat oven to 350°. Grease two 7 x 3½ x 2-inch loaf pans.

2. Mix flour with baking powder, salt, and lemon rind; set aside.

3. In large bowl, beat butter with sugar until light and fluffy. Add eggs, one at a time, beating well after each addition; beat until light and fluffy.

4. Stir in flour mixture alternately with milk and vanilla, beginning and ending with flour mixture; beat just until mixed. Stir in nuts. Spoon batter into prepared pans. Bake 45 minutes, or until cake tester inserted in center comes out clean.

5. Pour glaze evenly over breads as soon as they are removed from oven. Let cool in pan 10 minutes. Remove to wire rack; let cool completely. Freezes well.

GLAZE

¼ cup lemon juice   **⅓ cup sugar**

In small saucepan, combine lemon juice and sugar. Cook, stirring 1 minute, or until syrupy.

VENEZUELAN FLAN
Serves 6–8

1 cup sugar
4 eggs
1 cup plus 2 tablespoons light cream or half-and-half
2 teaspoons vanilla

1 14-ounce can sweetened condensed milk
½ teaspoon grated lime rind (optional)

1. Preheat oven to 350°. Melt sugar to a light, brown syrup in shallow baking pan with straight sides (an 8¼-inch round metal dish is good) on medium high heat. Do not stir; it only sticks to the spoon. Don't let it burn either, or it will taste bitter.

2. When melted, hold dish with pot holders and swirl all around pan so all sides are coated with syrup. Set aside.

3. Mix rest of ingredients with mixer and pour into caramel coated pan. Set flan in oven in pan set in one inch of hot water. Bake at 350° for one hour. Cool. Refrigerate until very cold.

4. When ready to serve, run small metal spatula or knife around edge of dish to loosen. Invert on platter with curved sides. Shake gently to release. The caramel makes a beautiful sauce all around custard.

Happy Holiday

COFFEE PUNCH
Serves 20

2 cups heavy cream, well chilled
2½ tablespoons powdered sugar
2½ teaspoons vanilla extract
Dash of cinnamon (optional)
1 quart coffee ice cream, cut in small chunks

1 quart vanilla or chocolate ice cream, cut in small chunks
2 quarts strong black coffee, well chilled

1. In medium-sized bowl, whip cream until almost stiff; add sugar and vanilla and continue whipping until cream holds its shape. This can be done 2 or 3 hours ahead and the whipped cream covered and refrigerated.

2. Put ice cream chunks into punch bowl, pour in coffee, and mix well. Top with spoonfuls of whipped cream.

AMBROSIA WITH ORANGE DRESSING
Serves 6

7 navel oranges
1½ cups grated fresh coconut or thawed frozen coconut

½ cup powdered or granulated sugar
⅓ cup orange juice

1. With sharp knife, peel oranges deeply enough to remove white membrane. Cut oranges into sections.

2. In 9-inch glass pie plate arrange layer of oranges. Add juice. Sprinkle with coconut and sugar. Repeat until oranges and coconut are used. Cover with plastic or foil. Refrigerate at least 2 hours. Serve with Orange Dressing.

VARIATION: Add 2 sliced bananas and ½ cup coarsely chopped pecans to the cut-up oranges. Mix lightly and layer with the coconut and sugar. Strawberries or seedless green grapes cut in half (about 1 cup) make a nice addition.

ORANGE DRESSING

½ cup salad dressing (optional)   ¼ teaspoon grated orange rind
¼ cup powdered sugar   ½ cup heavy cream, whipped
1 tablespoon orange juice

Combine salad dressing, sugar, orange juice, and rind; fold in whipped cream. Chill. Spoon over Ambrosia.

GREEN CHILI QUICHE
Serves 12

Pastry for 2-crust, 9-inch pie   ½ teaspoon salt
2 4-ounce cans chopped green   ¼ teaspoon pepper
    chilies, drained   2 tablespoons minced onion,
¼ cup flour   sautéed in 1 tablespoon
1 pound Swiss cheese, coarsely   butter
    grated (4 cups)   6 large eggs
1 cup grated Monterey Jack   Several drops hot pepper sauce
    cheese   2 cups hot half-and-half

1. Preheat oven to 325°. Press pastry evenly over bottom and sides of 15 x 12-inch jelly-roll pan. Spread chilies evenly over pastry.

2. In medium-sized bowl, mix flour with grated cheese, salt, pepper, and onion. Beat in eggs and half-and-half. Pour over chilies and bake 30 to 40 minutes, until top is lightly browned.

SAUSAGE PARTY CASSEROLE
Serves 10–12

2 pounds bulk pork sausage
1 cup chopped green pepper
¾ cup chopped onion
2½ cups coarsely chopped celery
4½ cups boiling water
½ teaspoon salt

2 packages dry chicken-noodle-
   soup mix
1 cup converted rice, uncooked
1 8-ounce can water chestnuts,
   drained and sliced

1. Brown sausage; pour off excess fat. Sauté green pepper, onion, and celery in the excess fat.
2. Combine soup mix with boiling water; stir in rice and simmer covered for 20 minutes. Add sausage, green pepper, onion, celery, salt, and water chestnuts. Pour into a 2-quart casserole. Bake at 375° for 20 minutes.

STRAWBERRY CREAM MOLD
Serves 12

1 6-ounce package raspberry-fla-
   vored gelatin
2 cups boiling water
2 cups crushed fresh
   strawberries
2 tablespoons lemon juice

½ cup sugar
⅛ teaspoon salt
¼ cup orange juice
1 cup heavy cream, whipped
1 cup sliced strawberries
Whole strawberries for garnish

1. Dissolve gelatin in boiling water. Cool slightly. Mix crushed strawberries, lemon juice, sugar, salt, and orange juice. Add to gelatin.
2. Chill until mixture is consistency of unbeaten egg whites. Then fold in the whipped cream and sliced strawberries. Pour into 8-cup mold and chill overnight. Garnish with whole strawberries. If you use a ring mold, fill center with whole strawberries when serving.

Fun Raising

> *Orange Cooler*
> *Fresh Melon Balls*
> *Pecan Waffles*
> *Canadian Bacon*
> *Coconut Krispies*

ORANGE COOLER
Serves 6
From Jeanne Wolf of ABC's "Good Morning, America"

1 cup sliced fresh strawberries
4 cups fresh orange juice
1 tablespoon honey

6 mint sprigs (optional)
1 cup chilled white grape juice (optional)

Blend strawberries, 1 cup orange juice, and honey in blender for 10 seconds. Mix in pitcher with remaining orange and grape juice. Serve in chilled glasses. Garnish with mint sprig.

VARIATION: 2 bananas can be used in place of strawberries.

FRESH MELON BALLS
Serves 8

1 cantaloupe melon
1 honeydew melon

½ teaspoon freshly grated ginger
1 tablespoon fresh lime juice

1. With melon scoop, carve cantaloupe and honeydew into balls.

2. Sprinkle ginger and lime juice over melon balls. Toss gently. Chill at least one hour.

3. Arrange in serving bowl. Place fancy toothpicks nearby so guests can spear melon balls.

PECAN WAFFLES
Makes 10–12 waffles

2½ cups sifted flour
1½ tablespoons brown or white
 sugar
4 teaspoons baking powder
¾ teaspoon salt

2 beaten eggs
2¼ cups milk
½ cup oil
¼ cup finely chopped pecans

1. Sift flour, sugar, baking powder, and salt.
2. Combine eggs, milk, and oil; add pecans. Add to dry ingredients just before baking. Mix just until moistened. (Batter is thin.)
3. Pour onto preheated baker. Serve with strawberries or peaches, sugar, and nutmeg.

CANADIAN BACON

1 whole Canadian bacon

3 tablespoons pickling spice

In large saucepan, cover bacon with water. Add pickling spice and bring to a boil. Simmer gently 1 hour. Cool slightly and slice. Arrange on platter.

COCONUT KRISPIES
Makes 10 dozen

1 cup sugar
1 cup brown sugar
1 cup margarine
1 cup salad oil
1 egg
1 teaspoon vanilla
1 teaspoon salt
1 teaspoon cream of tartar

1 teaspoon soda
3½ cups flour
1 cup Rice Krispies
1 cup coconut flakes
1 cup oatmeal (either quick or
 regular)
½ to 1 cup nuts, chopped

Preheat oven to 350°. Mix all ingredients together, adding Rice Krispies last. Drop heaping teaspoons of mixture on ungreased cookie sheet. (Use 3 or 4 sheets to go faster.) Bake for 12 to 15 minutes; I leave them in 14 minutes.

NOTE: Since this recipe makes a lot of cookies, freeze dough in several portions, and bake cookies periodically without the mess of *making* the dough. Baked cookies freeze well too.

Florida Favorite

ORANGE FRAPPÉ
Serves 6

1 12-ounce can frozen orange juice
1 quart cold water

1 pint lemon sherbert
6 slices of orange for garnish

Mix frozen orange juice with cold water. Chill. To serve pour ½ cup orange juice into 6 glasses. Top with 1 or 2 scoops lemon sherbert and swirl into orange juice. Garnish with orange slices.

FABULOUS CHEESE CASSEROLE
Serves 6–8

8 slices white bread (regular, not thin sliced)
2 cups shredded sharp Cheddar cheese
¼ cup melted butter
5 eggs
3 cups milk

½ teaspoon salt
¼ teaspoon pepper
1 teaspoon dry mustard
1 teaspoon Worcestershire sauce
6 strips bacon, cut in half

1. Trim crusts from bread. Cut each piece in three strips. Fit strips together tightly in bottom of greased 2-quart flat baking dish.

Pour melted butter over bread. Sprinkle with half the cheese. Repeat with rest of bread and cheese.

2. Beat eggs and milk together and stir in the salt, pepper, and mustard. Pour this over bread and cheese. Lay bacon on top. Refrigerate overnight.

3. The next morning bake, uncovered, at 350° for 50 to 55 minutes until puffed and firm in center. Remove from oven just after guests sit down; otherwise it may tend to sink. (Tastes just as great, but doesn't look as glamorous.) Garnish with sprig of parsley in center.

VARIATION: Substitute ½ pound lightly browned sausage for the bacon. Sprinkle sausage on first layer of bread. Cover with remaining ingredients.

RATATOUILLE
Serves 12

Delicious cold, hot, or at room temperature. This recipe makes a lot, but I just crave it. You can eat it all day long and not get fat! I freeze lunch-size portions for myself.

2 pounds eggplant (2 medium eggplants) peeled and cut into 1-inch cubes

2 pounds zucchini (4 large zucchini), unpeeled, cut into ½-inch slices

3 pounds tomatoes (about 4–6 tomatoes), peeled and quartered

2 teaspoons salt

½ cup flour

Olive oil (about 1 cup)

2 large onions, chopped

2 garlic cloves, crushed

2 green peppers, cut in strips

Pinch of sugar

2 teaspoons salt

Freshly ground pepper to taste

½ cup chopped parsley

2 teaspoons dried basil

Pinch of marjoram, oregano, thyme

6 tablespoons freshly grated Parmesan cheese

1 tablespoon catsup

1 tablespoon chili sauce

1 tablespoon tomato puree

1 tablespoon tomato paste

1. Toss eggplant and zucchini together with 2 teaspoons salt. Let stand in bowl for 30 minutes. Drain, rinse and dry vegetables on paper towels. Shake vegetables with flour in paper bag to coat.

2. Sauté eggplant and zucchini in hot olive oil until golden in large skillet. Set aside in bowl. In same skillet sauté onions, garlic and green peppers in several tablespoons of hot oil. Add tomatoes, sugar, salt, and pepper and cook 5 minutes longer.

3. Return eggplant and zucchini to skillet along with rest of ingredients. Mix gently and simmer uncovered for 45 minutes or until most of liquid has evaporated.

4. Add to the above the puree, paste, catsup and chili sauce, or any combination of these four. They aren't necessary, but I like the snappy taste. Sprinkle with Parmesan cheese.

MANGO BREAD

2 cups flour	¾ cup oil
1½ cups sugar	½ cup raisins
2 teaspoons baking soda	½ cup chopped nuts
2 teaspoons cinnamon	2 cups diced mangoes
½ teaspoon salt	1 tablespoon lime juice
3 eggs, slightly beaten	(optional)

Stir together flour, sugar, baking soda, cinnamon and salt. Stir in eggs and oil. Add rest of ingredients and pour into one buttered loaf pan (9 x 5 x 2½ inches) or three pans (7 x 3½ x 2 inches). Bake one hour at 350°. Bread slices better if baked a day ahead. Freezes beautifully.

CREAMY RICE PUDDING
Serves 8

1 cup cooked white rice	½ teaspoon grated lemon peel
1⅔ cups milk	½ teaspoon ground coriander
¼ teaspoon salt	(optional)
3 egg yolks	2 teaspoons vanilla
½ cup sugar	1 inch cinnamon stick
1 envelope unflavored gelatin	1 cup whipping cream
1 teaspoon grated orange peel	

1. Mix cooked rice, ⅓ cup of milk, and salt in small covered saucepan and simmer until rice absorbs the milk.

2. In heavy 1-quart saucepan, beat egg yolks and sugar until light. Beat in remaining 1⅓ cups milk. Sprinkle gelatin evenly over egg mixture. Cook over low heat, stirring constantly, until gelatin is completely dissolved and mixture thickens and coats a spoon (about 15 minutes). Do not boil.

3. Combine rice (which has absorbed the milk) with egg mixture. Stir in orange and lemon peels, coriander, vanilla, and cinnamon stick. Refrigerate 30 minutes. Remove cinnamon stick.

4. Beat cream until thick. Fold into cooled rice mixture. Spoon into 1-quart mold; cover and refrigerate for 4 hours or until set. Unmold on a cake plate, and garnish with orange sections.

3
Just for Fun

Let's Participate
The Family Tree
Michelle's Favorite
Derby Day

Godzilla à la King

"We don't encourage dating on campus," once said Dr. V. Raymond Edman, president of Wheaton College. "We don't have to," he continued, with a wink and a knowing grin.

Most women I know don't need encouragement to celebrate on holidays. I mean, who doesn't get excited on Christmas and Thanksgiving and birthdays? That's easy. But what about the months and months of monotony in between?

I believe it really doesn't take more money to make life exciting, but, rather, just a little imagination and the desire. Your *attitude* can transform tonight's dinner into a happening. You might try one of these ideas. It might just spin around the Grouch of the Day, whoever he or she might be.

1. *Find an occasion.* Celebrate Sundays, fun days, half birthdays. Celebrate if Rover has a birthday. Celebrate Godzilla, haircuts, new jeans. Celebrate seasons, weekends, report cards. Celebrate Mommy's raise. Celebrate braces on, braces off, Junior's home run. Celebrate if Daddy comes home early, or if Daddy comes *home!* If Daddy made a sale or fixed the drain or mowed the yard. For rain or health or carwash . . . celebrate.

2. *Find a new location.* Try the bedroom or the den for a change. I remember eating a Japanese dinner on our living-room floor, with all of us sitting around the coffee table on pillows covered with brightly colored shawls. My family ate everything not tied down, including the vegetables. (Wonder of wonders!) The cleanup after the chopstick fiasco was another story. Next oriental meal goes outside.

3. *Exchange the seasons.* Make a memory with a new twist. Decorate for Thanksgiving in February. Or a Fourth of July picnic in the dead of winter. Color Easter eggs in August. I guarantee you'll be the only one in your block.

4. *Name your guest of honor.* With icing in a tube, add the name of your special guest on the cake. Or on the pie. Or with a simple cake-decorating kit, decorate the meatloaf with mayonnaise. Add a dash of sprinkles, grated carrot, or slivers of stuffed olives to make a design.

5. *Slice it thin.* For a change, thinly slice eggs, tomatoes, broccoli, melon, whatever. Fan out the slices in a pattern on a salad plate, as in the French tradition.

6. *Color it blue.* Eat in vivid technicolor instead of black and white. Use food coloring creatively. Dress the table with wild flowers or even weeds. (Be wary of ragweed!) Help the children to make place cards and silly hats. Drape crepe-paper streamers from the chandelier to each plate.

7. *Present it differently.* Display your salad mold on a cake stand. Serve buffet-style from pots on the stove. Instead of a dinner plate, use saucers and bowls, in the Japanese manner. Pile fruit salad or sherbert balls (cut with melon scoop) in your treasured goblets and stand them on pretty saucers.

8. *Rename the unpopular.* When I was growing up, I probably would have acquired a taste earlier for certain foods if their awful-sounding names had been more tantalizingly identified. You can enlist the children's help for new names for foods they might consider unpopular like yogurt, squash, sour cream, rutabagas, parsnips, and prunes. (No guarantees, but it just might help.)

9. *Dress up the cook!*

Let's Participate

Beef "Fun-Do" with Sauces
Fluffy Rice
Three-Ring-Circus Salad
Hot-Fudge-and-Peanut-Butter Sundaes

BEEF "FUN-DO" WITH SAUCES
Serves 6

2 pounds tender lean steak (filet
  has the least waste)
2 to 3 cups salad oil

1 stick butter (optional)
1 or 2 garlic cloves, cut in half

1. Early in day, remove all fat and cut beef into 1-inch cubes. Arrange on serving platter and cover with plastic wrap. Refrigerate.

2. At serving time, fill fondue pot or minifryer with salad oil to 2-inch depth; add butter if you desire. Add 2 cut garlic halves. (To save time, heat oil on stove and then pour into fondue pot placed over heat source.)

3. Each person can cook his or her own meat cubes at table with long-handled fork. Children love to spear and cook their meat in bubbling oil. Cook about 30 to 45 seconds for medium. Reheat oil on range if necessary.

4. Serve several sauces in center of table, so the family can dip their cooked cubes in favorite sauce. Dip meat in sauce with table fork, so fondue fork can be cooking next cube in pot.

CREAM CHEESE-CHILI SAUCE

1½ teaspoons green chilies
  (canned)
½ onion, minced
1 clove garlic, minced
¼ cup olive oil

¼ cup wine vinegar
¼ teaspoon salt
2 tablespoons crumbled cream
  or farmer cheese

Mix all ingredients together except cheese and let stand for several hours. Stir in cheese and serve.

SWEET-AND-SOUR APRICOT SAUCE

½ of 12-ounce jar apricot   ¼ teaspoon ground ginger
    preserves   Dash of salt
2 teaspoons white vinegar

In a small saucepan combine all ingredients. Place over moderate heat and bring mixture to a boil. Reduce heat to moderately low and cook 2 minutes, stirring constantly. Cool.

MUSTARD SAUCE

2 tablespoons Dijon mustard   ¼ cup mayonnaise

Combine ingredients. *Voilà!* This sauce may also be used for steaks.

SAUCE INDIENNE

¼ cup mayonnaise or salad   1 teaspoon curry powder
    dressing   ¼ teaspoon onion powder
2 tablespoons chili sauce   Dash cayenne pepper

Combine all ingredients and mix well. Cover and chill.

FLUFFY RICE
Serves 6

1 10¾-ounce can chicken broth,   ¼ teaspoon salt
    undiluted   1 teaspoon butter
1 cup uncooked regular rice   ⅓ cup finely chopped walnuts

Mix chicken broth with water to equal 2 cups. Combine with rice and salt in saucepan. Bring to a boil; stir once, reduce heat, cover tightly, and simmer 15 minutes. Remove from heat. Let rice set (covered) for 5 minutes. Add butter and chopped walnuts, stir lightly, and serve.

TIP: For that perfect dish of rice, each grain separate and slightly *al dente,* simply cook rice in a little butter before adding water and salt. Fat coats the grains and keeps them from sticking together.

THREE-RING-CIRCUS SALAD

Canned pineapple rings   Lettuce leaves
Grated Cheddar cheese   Maraschino cherries

Arrange 3 pineapple rings overlapping on each lettuce-lined salad plate. Sprinkle grated Cheddar cheese lightly over top. Garnish with cherries in hole of each pineapple slice.

HOT-FUDGE-AND-PEANUT-BUTTER SUNDAES
Serves 6

1 6-ounce package semisweet   ½ cup sugar
   chocolate chips   ½ cup peanut butter
1 cup milk   1 quart ice cream

Mix chocolate chips, milk, and sugar in small saucepan and bring to boil, stirring constantly. Stir boiling mixture slowly into peanut butter. Serve over ice cream scoops.

The Family Tree

PORTRAIT PATTIES
Serves 6

1½ pounds ground beef
4 slices raw bacon, cut up fine
1 tablespoon Worcestershire
    sauce
6 slices white or yellow cheese

Pitted black olives, sliced
Stuffed green olives, sliced
Pimentos cut in strips
1 small loaf French bread, cut in
    ½-inch slices and buttered

1. Mix beef, bacon, and Worcestershire sauce together and shape into 6 patties. Place patties in salted, hot skillet. Fry meat patties to desired doneness.

2. Place cheese slice on each patty, covering entire surface. Make faces with olives for eyes, pimento strips for mouths and eyebrows. Make eyes crossed, or looking up, mouths turned up and down. Or you can cut out a face in the cheese slice and just place it on the hamburger.

3. Toast buttered-bread slices in oven under broiler for a minute or two, place portrait patty on top. Serve all the portraits on a large platter, garnished with parsley, if desired. The children can make menus for each place setting.

BROCCOLI CASSEROLE
Serves 6

1 package frozen broccoli
(thawed)
¼ cup onion, chopped
¼ cup celery, chopped
4 tablespoons butter
1 8-ounce jar Cheese Whiz

½ 10-ounce can cream of mushroom soup
¾ cup Minute Rice (uncooked)
¼ cup chopped almonds
(optional)
½ cup bread crumbs

Sauté onion and celery in 2 tablespoons of butter. Add broccoli and cook 5 minutes. Mix together all ingredients except remaining butter and bread crumbs. Pour into buttered casserole. Melt butter in small skillet. Stir in bread crumbs. Sprinkle over top of casserole. Bake uncovered at 350° for 45 minutes.

SITA'S NO-KNEAD WHOLE-WHEAT BREAD
Makes one loaf

4 teaspoons dry yeast
⅔ cup lukewarm water
2 teaspoons honey
5 cups whole-wheat flour
3 tablespoons molasses
½ tablespoon salt

⅓ cup wheat germ
1¾ cups lukewarm water
1 tablespoon butter, melted
1 tablespoon sesame seeds
(unhulled)

1. Butter loaf pan (9¼ x 5½ x 2¾-inch), taking care to grease the corners well.
2. Sprinkle yeast over ⅔ cup of lukewarm (110°) water. Add honey. Stir to dissolve yeast. Warm whole-wheat flour by placing it in 250° oven for 20 minutes.
3. Stir molasses into yeast mixture and add warmed flour, salt, wheat germ, and finally 1¾ cups lukewarm water. The dough will be sticky.
4. Turn dough into pan. No kneading is necessary. Hold spatula under cold water, and smooth dough in pan. Brush melted butter over dough, and sprinkle sesame seeds on top. Let loaf rise to top

of pan in warm, draft-free place. Meanwhile, preheat oven to 400°.
    5. Bake in preheated oven for 30 to 40 minutes, or until crust is brown and sides of loaf are firm and crusty. Set pan on rack to cool for about ten minutes. Remove loaf from pan and cool completely on rack before slicing.

WATERMELON SPARKLER
Serves 8

½ watermelon cut into 8 serving   8 sparklers
    pieces

    Place watermelon on serving tray. When ready to serve, place lighted sparklers in top of melon, and present to delighted guests. (Watch your tablecloth!)

Michelle's Favorite

> *Spaghetti with Cheese-Stuffed Meatballs*
> *Bibb Lettuce-and-Tomato Salad*
> *Toasted Bun Sticks*
> *Orange Freeze*

SPAGHETTI WITH CHEESE-STUFFED MEATBALLS
Serves 8

SAUCE

2 tablespoons salad or olive oil
1 cup chopped onion
2 cloves garlic, crushed
1 cup grated carrots or 1 cup chopped celery
1 teaspoon salt
½ teaspoon pepper
1 can undiluted beef bouillon
½ cup red grape juice (optional)
1 teaspoon dried basil

1 teaspoon oregano
1 2-pound, 3-ounce-can tomatoes, undrained
2 6-ounce cans tomato paste
2 tablespoons parsley
1 teaspoon sugar
2 tablespoons Worcestershire sauce
Dash of nutmeg

MEATBALLS

2 pounds ground chuck
1 2¼-ounce can deviled ham (optional)
½ pound Italian sausage
¼ cup dry bread crumbs
2 cloves garlic, crushed
¼ pound Cheddar cheese or mozzarella

2 teaspoons salt
½ teaspoon pepper
2 eggs, slightly beaten
½ cup milk
1 teaspoon dried basil leaves
½ cup chopped parsley
1 pound spaghetti or vermicelli
Grated Parmesan cheese

1. The day before, make sauce. In hot oil in 6-quart Dutch oven, sauté onion, garlic, and celery 5 minutes.

2. Add remaining sauce ingredients; mix well. Bring to boiling, stirring. Reduce heat; simmer, covered and stirring occasionally, for 2 hours. Set aside.

3. While sauce is cooking, make meatballs: In large bowl, combine remaining ingredients, except cheeses and spaghetti. Cut Cheddar or mozzarella cheese into ½-inch cubes. With moistened hands, shape mixture into meatballs 1½ inches in diameter, with cheese cubes in center.

4. Broil meatballs on all sides on cookie sheet with rim, shaking sheet occasionally. Add meatballs to sauce; simmer covered, 30 minutes longer. Refrigerate.

5. One half hour before serving, reheat sauce and cook spaghetti as directed; drain. Mound spaghetti on large round platter; top with meatballs. Pour sauce over all. Sprinkle with Parmesan cheese.

TIP: It's easy to keep pasta at piping-hot temperature. If you will be using the pasta shortly after cooking, return the drained pasta to the empty cooking pan, add butter, then cover the pasta to keep it warm. If the pasta won't be used for 20 minutes or more, drain it in a colander and place the colander over a pan containing a small amount of boiling water. Coat pasta with three to four tablespoons butter or margarine (for six servings) to keep it from sticking. Cover the colander.

BIBB LETTUCE-AND-TOMATO SALAD
Serves 4

2 heads Bibb lettuce, torn in   ½ teaspoon salt
    pieces and chilled   ⅓ cup salad oil
2 tomatoes, cut in wedges   ⅔ cup tarragon vinegar
1 clove garlic, crushed

Mix garlic, salt, oil and vinegar together with a fork. Spoon over lettuce and tomatoes in salad bowl and toss. Serve on chilled salad plates.

TOASTED BUN STICKS
Serves 6

3 hot-dog buns   **½ cup Italian salad dressing**

Preheat oven to 350°. Cut each bun into 4 lengthwise sticks, making 12 sticks. Brush generously with salad dressing. Bake on cookie sheet for 15 to 18 minutes until tops are lightly browned.

ORANGE FREEZE
Serves 6

2 pints orange sherbert   **2 large oranges, peeled and**
4 eggs   **seeded**
                                              Orange wedges for garnish

Put all ingredients in blender. Whirl until smooth. Pour into 6 glasses (frosted in freezer) and garnish with orange wedges.

Derby Day

Pinwheel Cheese Meatloaf
Easy Rice Casserole
Peas in Cream
Brown Derby Gingerbread
with Butterscotch Sauce

PINWHEEL CHEESE MEATLOAF
Serves 6

1½ pounds lean ground beef
¾ cup cracker crumbs (or bread crumbs)
½ cup finely chopped onion
1 egg
1 teaspoon salt
1 teaspoon prepared horseradish (optional)
½ teaspoon oregano
⅛ teaspoon pepper
1 teaspoon Worcestershire sauce
1 8-ounce can tomato sauce
1½ cups shredded Cheddar cheese
½ cup shredded Cheddar cheese (for topping)

1. Combine beef, cracker crumbs, onion, egg, salt, horseradish, oregano, pepper, and Worcestershire sauce and ½ can of tomato sauce. Mix well and on waxed paper or foil shape into flat rectangle about 14 inches by 10 inches.

2. Sprinkle cheese evenly over meat mixture up to 1 inch of edges. Roll up from shorter side like jelly roll, and press ends to seal.

3. Remove from paper or foil. Transfer to shallow baking dish, seam side down. Bake at 350° for 45 minutes.

4. Drain off excess fat. Pour remaining tomato sauce over roll and bake 15 minutes more. Sprinkle top with ½ cup shredded cheese. Let stand a few minutes to melt.

EASY RICE CASSEROLE
Serves 6

1 cup long-grain rice	1 package onion-soup mix
3 cups water	4 tablespoons butter

Mix together and bake covered for 1 hour at 325°.

PEAS IN CREAM
Serves 6–8

2 10-ounce packages frozen peas	½ cup water
2 teaspoons sugar	2 tablespoons butter
2 teaspoons salt	Pepper to taste
4 green onions, chopped	¾ cup light cream

Cook peas, sugar, salt, and onion in water for 5 minutes. Drain. Add butter, pepper and cream. Heat through but don't cook.

VARIATION: Add 1 cup thinly sliced cooked carrots with butter and cream.

BROWN DERBY GINGERBREAD WITH
BUTTERSCOTCH SAUCE

½ cup vegetable shortening	2 eggs
½ cup sugar	1 cup boiling water
2½ cups flour	2 teaspoons ground ginger
1 cup molasses	1 teaspoon cinnamon
2 teaspoons baking soda	½ teaspoon ground cloves
½ teaspoon salt	½ teaspoon allspice

Preheat oven to 350°. Mix together all ingredients and pour into buttered 9 x 13-inch baking pan. Bake for 1 hour. Serve hot or cold, topped with butterscotch sauce. A scoop of vanilla ice cream takes you into ecstasy!

BUTTERSCOTCH SAUCE
Makes 1¼ cups

¼ cup butter
¾ cup brown sugar
¼ cup coffee cream or evaporated milk

2 tablespoons light corn syrup
Dash of salt

Melt butter in saucepan over low heat. Stir in brown sugar, corn syrup and cream; cook to boiling point. Then remove from heat, and cool slightly. Serve warm or cold.

4
Time to Reconcile

Building Bridges
Peace Pipe
Wood Elevator
Let's Pull Together

Stormy Weather

Reconcile, according to Webster, means "to restore to friendship, compatibility, or harmony."

For me, life's darkest moments come when I am estranged from someone I love. If I am out of fellowship with Charlie or a dear friend, I am absolutely miserable until we're reconciled; that is, "restore[d] to friendship, compatibility, or harmony."

Occasionally Charlie and I have an out-and-out disagreement. Sometimes it's my fault. Sometimes it's his. Sometimes it's both. Not that it matters much when we're both miserable. How I hate those days.

One morning recently, we had a disagreement as Charlie was leaving for work. We began arguing, and then suddenly we were shouting. I could feel bitterness rising in me, and I wanted to hit him with the greasy frying pan. As he stormed out the door, I had a moment of remorse and shouted after him, "I hope we don't die today and spend our last day like this."

He just drove away, stonefaced.

Back at the kitchen sink I thought, *What an indomitable grouch. I can't stand to look at him tonight, much less cook for him.* I stormed out of the kitchen.

In my wretched state I remembered I had forgotten to kiss my girls good-bye. Later that morning, I was curt to a friend on the phone. I snapped at the mailman. Finally, I realized my anger was only making *me* more miserable.

I decided to gather myself together and tackle my plan for the day. I asked myself, *What about supper when Charlie comes home tonight? Regardless of how we feel, our whole family will be hungry at suppertime.*

I considered my options:

1. Let Charlie cook his own supper.
2. Cook his supper and throw it at him.
3. Cook his supper and we'd all eat in silence. (The only problem is that Charlie would eat his, but I couldn't eat mine.)
4. Reconcile.

After carefully considering the first three alternatives, I chose the last option, to reconcile. I knew I couldn't reconcile in my own strength. I was too mad. So, I read the Bible.

I turned to 1 Corinthians 13, the "love chapter." It showed me the way back: "Love endures long *and* is patient and kind; love never is envious *nor* boils over with jealousy. . . . Love [God's love in us] does not insist on its own rights *or* its own way, *for* it is not self-seeking; it is not touchy *or* fretful *or* resentful; it takes no account of the evil done to it—pays no attention to a suffered wrong."

I knew we couldn't settle our argument before we ate, since we both are more irritable when we're hungry and tired. But I could forget whose fault it was, and fix *supper,* not the blame.

The matter was not yet resolved, but with God's love in control, I could function joyfully. I could set the scene for reconciliation, a table alive with fresh flowers and color. Preparing his favorite dish, I could convey the message, "Let's be cozy again. I want to meet your needs. I *love* you."

And it worked. Charlie met me halfway. Our insurmountable problem seemed to melt away.

The hurt of being separated from a loved one is surpassed only by the joy of being reconciled to that person.

Love never fails.

Building Bridges

BAKED BARBECUED BRISKET OF BEEF
Serves 8
Leftovers make luscious sandwiches.

1 lean brisket of beef (4 to 5 pounds)
1 medium-sized onion, finely chopped
1 clove garlic, minced
2 tablespoons vegetable oil
1 tablespoon chili powder
½ cup catsup
½ cup tomato sauce
½ cup cider or white vinegar
¼ cup lemon juice
2 tablespoons Worcestershire sauce
¼ cup firmly packed brown sugar
1 tablespoon prepared mustard
1 teaspoon celery seeds
1 teaspoon cumin seed, crushed
2 tablespoons corn syrup

1. Preheat oven to 350°. Sauté onion and garlic in oil in a large saucepan until golden, about 10 minutes. Add remaining ingredients and bring to a boil. Lower heat, simmer uncovered, stirring often, for 30 minutes.

2. Center a 24-inch length of 18-inch heavy-duty foil in a 13 x 9 x 2-inch baking pan. Place brisket on center of foil. Pour sauce over meat. Bring ends of foil together evenly; fold over and continue folding down to top of meat. Fold sides up to make a neat sealed package. Bake package in pan for 3 hours or until meat is tender.

3. Remove from oven. Carefully open foil; lift meat to heated serving platter. Pour sauce from foil into sauce dish. Skim off excess fat. Serve sauce with meat.

BAKED POTATOES
Serves 6

6 large baking potatoes   6 tablespoons butter
Salt water

Soak potatoes in salted cold water for 15 minutes. Dry and pierce each potato with fork. Bake at 350° for 1 hour. With sharp knife make a cross in top of potato. Squeeze to puff open. Place a thin slice of butter across opening. Serve steaming hot.

OVEN ASPARAGUS
Serves 6

1½ pounds asparagus   Lemon wedges (optional)
3 tablespoons butter or less Paprika (optional)
Salt and pepper

1. Rinse asparagus and trim each stalk to about 5 inches long. Put asparagus tips in a shallow baking dish in 1 layer and sprinkle them with salt, pepper, and 3 tablespoons water.

2. Dot asparagus with 3 tablespoons butter cut into small pieces (for dieters, less). Cover dish tightly with aluminum foil, and bake at 325° for 30 minutes.

3. Place in serving dish and pour pan juices over top. Dip edges of lemon wedges in paprika and arrange around dish, cut side up.

ONION AND GREEN BEAN SALAD
Serves 6

2 mild-flavored onions (such as   2 tablespoons white vinegar
   Bermuda), sliced   ¼ teaspoon sweet basil
1 tablespoon sugar   ¼ teaspoon salt

2 10-ounce packages frozen green beans
5 slices bacon
⅓ cup salad oil

Dash of cayenne pepper
2 heads Bibb lettuce, washed and dried

1. Separate onion slices into rings. Place in medium bowl; sprinkle with sugar.

2. Cook beans as label directs; drain. Cool; toss with onion rings. Chill for at least 1 hour, stirring occasionally. Cook bacon; crumble and reserve.

3. At serving time, divide lettuce leaves among individual salad plates. In small bowl, mix together salad oil and remaining ingredients. Pour oil mixture over salad ingredients and toss gently. Pile on lettuce leaves.

HEAVENLY HASH
Serves 8

½ cup raw white rice
1 8¾-ounce can pineapple tidbits, drained
1 cup miniature marshmallows
10 maraschino cherries, halved (⅓ cup)

1 cup heavy cream, whipped, or 1-pint container Cool Whip
1 teaspoon vanilla
2 tablespoons maraschino cherry juice
Slivered almonds

1. Cook rice as package label directs for softer rice. Refrigerate until well chilled.

2. In large bowl, combine pineapple tidbits, chilled rice, marshmallows, and cherries; stir until well combined. Refrigerate covered overnight.

3. One hour before serving, stir cherry juice into rice mixture. Fold in whipped cream or Cool Whip just until combined. Spoon into pretty bowl and refrigerate. Sprinkle almonds on top just before serving.

Peace Pipe

Glazed Stuffed Pork Chops
Lemon Zucchini
Tomato and Onion Vinaigrette
Hot Herb Bread
Coconut Cream Pie

GLAZED STUFFED PORK CHOPS
Serves 4

4 2-inch-thick loin pork chops
(slit a 2-inch pocket in fatty
side for stuffing)
2 tablespoons butter
½ cup chopped onions
½ cup chopped celery and a few
tops
⅓ cup orange juice or hot water
1 cup stuffing mix
¼ teaspoon salt
¼ teaspoon pepper
¼ teaspoon thyme
¼ teaspoon sage (optional)
2 tablespoons snipped parsley
¼ cup toasted chopped almonds
or pecans
1 orange cut into small bits
(optional)
Canned apricots for garnish

1. Brown chops in hot fat. Salt and pepper both sides. Remove from pan. Sauté onions and celery in butter. Stir in rest of ingredients.

2. Put stuffing in chop pockets and place in buttered baking dish. Add 2 tablespoons hot water. Sprinkle chops with extra salt and pepper. Cover tightly with foil and bake 1½ hours at 325°.

3. Remove foil and baste with glaze. Bake uncovered 15 minutes longer. Arrange on platter and garnish with apricot halves centered with maraschino cherries, if desired.

GLAZE

1 can apricot nectar
4 teaspoons Worcestershire
sauce

½ tablespoon cornstarch
Dash of cinnamon

Combine and cook until thickened. Brush on both sides of chops.

LEMON ZUCCHINI
Serves 4

3 large zucchini
¼ cup butter
1 small onion, chopped

1 teaspoon grated lemon peel
2 tablespoons lemon juice

1. Wash zucchini, cut in ¼-inch slices, and cook for a few minutes in small amount of boiling salted water or chicken broth until tender. Drain.

2. Sauté onion in butter just until soft, not brown. Mix with lemon peel and juice and pour over cooked zucchini.

TOMATO AND ONION VINAIGRETTE
Serves 4

2 large ripe tomatoes, sliced
1 red onion, peeled and sliced
thin
1 tablespoon chopped parsley
1 teaspoon dried sweet basil
1 clove garlic, minced

5 tablespoons salad oil
2 tablespoons red wine vinegar
Dash of salt and pepper
2 small heads Bibb lettuce,
washed and dried

1. Separate onion slices into rings and arrange on top of tomato slices. Blend rest of ingredients together in blender. Pour over onions and tomatoes and chill until serving time.

2. To serve, arrange lettuce leaves on individual salad plates. Pile salad on top and drizzle dressing over all.

HOT HERB BREAD

1 loaf Italian bread (about 14
   inches)
½ cup soft butter
1 tablespoon chopped parsley
Dash of oregano

½ teaspoon dried dill weed
   (optional)
1 clove garlic, minced
Grated Parmesan cheese

Cut bread diagonally into 1 inch slices. Blend butter, parsley, oregano, dill and garlic. Put bread slices together again with butter mixture in between. Wrap loaf with foil, boat fashion, twisting ends and leaving top open. Sprinkle top liberally with cheese and more parsley flakes. Heat in hot oven (400°) until top browns, about 10 minutes.

COCONUT CREAM PIE
Serves 8

1 9-inch pastry shell, baked and
   cooled
⅔ cup sugar
½ teaspoon salt
2½ tablespoons cornstarch
1 tablespoon flour
2¾ cups milk

3 egg yolks, slightly beaten
1 tablespoon vanilla
1 cup moist shredded coconut
3 egg whites, beaten stiff
   (optional)
½ cup heavy cream, whipped

1. Mix sugar, salt, cornstarch and flour in saucepan. Stir in milk slowly and cook over medium heat, stirring constantly, until mixture thickens and begins to boil. Boil for one minute. Remove from heat.

2. Slowly pour half of mixture into egg yolks, stirring constantly. Then blend egg-yolk mixture into remaining hot pudding in saucepan. Boil one more minute, stirring constantly. Remove from heat and stir in vanilla. Cool slightly.

3. Beat egg whites with 2 tablespoons sugar until stiff and fold into pudding mixture. Gently stir in ½ cup coconut. Sprinkle ½ cup coconut on bottom of cooled baked pie shell. Pour pudding on top and chill.

4. Sweeten whipped cream with 2 teaspoons powdered sugar, if desired, and spread on top of pie. Sprinkle with coconut.

VARIATION: For BANANA CREAM PIE omit coconut. Line pie crust with 3 sliced bananas and pour pudding on top.

Mood Elevator

CRISPY ROAST CHICKEN
Serves 4

1 4- to 5-pound chicken	Juice of half a lemon
½ cup butter	¼ cup celery leaves
½ teaspoon salt	1 onion
Freshly ground pepper	1 tablespoon of mayonnaise
¼ teaspoon ginger	(optional)

1. Preheat oven to 325°. Rinse chicken and dry with paper towel. Melt butter in small saucepan and pour clarified butter into cup, leaving butter residue in bottom of pan.

2. Rub body cavity with 1 tablespoon clarified butter, ginger, salt, pepper, and lemon juice. Rub outside of chicken with cut lemon half and drizzle with 2 tablespoons of clarified butter. Put celery leaves and quartered onion in cavity. Tie legs together. Rub mayonnaise over chicken, if you desire, for a crisp brown crust.

3. Place breast side down in shallow roasting pan. Bake for 2 hours (about 30 minutes per pound), turning chicken on its back after 40 minutes. Baste every 20 minutes with remaining clarified butter. Test for doneness by piercing skin to see if juices run clear.

PINEAPPLE GLAZE

½ of 6-ounce can frozen pineapple juice concentrate,
thawed
2 tablespoons firmly packed
brown sugar

2 tablespoons white vinegar
¼ cup honey

In small bowl, combine all ingredients and blend well. Brush roast chicken with glaze several times during last 30 minutes of baking time.

STUFFED BAKED POTATOES
Serves 8

8 large baking potatoes
4 tablespoons butter
2 cups grated sharp Cheddar
cheese
2 egg yolks, beaten (optional)
½ cup sour cream
3 tablespoons finely chopped
onions
1 clove garlic, minced
1 teaspoon salt

Dash of cayenne pepper
(optional)
¼ teaspoon white or black
pepper
2 tablespoons melted butter
1 tablespoon chopped parsley for
garnish
Paprika
4 slices bacon, cooked and
crumbled (optional)

1. Wash potatoes; dry; rub with oil; prick skins. Bake at 400° for 1 hour or until done. Sauté onions and garlic in butter until tender; set aside.

2. Cut ¼ inch slice off top of baked potatoes and scoop out pulp, leaving shells intact about ¼ inch thick. Mash pulp and add sautéed onions and garlic, egg yolks mixed with sour cream and seasonings. Beat well and restuff potatoes.

3. If serving potatoes at once, brush tops with 2 tablespoons melted butter and slide under broiler for moment to brown. Sprinkle with paprika, parsley and crumbled bacon. (The stuffed potatoes may be kept at room temperature several hours before serving.

When ready to serve, brush potatoes with 2 tablespoons melted butter and bake at 400° for 20 minutes or until brown.)

TIP: Freeze extra potatoes in plastic bag. To reheat frozen potatoes, place on cookie sheet in 400° oven for 45 minutes.

CREAMED SPINACH
Serves 4–6
Supereasy!

2 packages chopped frozen spinach, thawed and drained on
   a paper towel

1 cup sour cream
1 envelope cheese-garlic or garlic dressing mix

Add sour cream and envelope of dry dressing mix to drained spinach. Heat gently until bubbly, about 5 minutes.

PARMESAN ROLL-UPS
Makes 16 rolls
Have the kids make these!

1 package refrigerated crescent
   rolls
¼ cup creamy Caesar salad
   dressing

1 cup herb or cheese-flavored
   croutons, crushed
Grated Parmesan cheese

1. Preheat oven to 375°. Unroll and separate dough to form 4 rectangles, pinching perforations to seal. Brush each generously with salad dressing. Cut each rectangle crosswise and lengthwise to form four smaller rectangles.

2. With wide spatula, lift each rectangle and invert onto crushed croutons, pressing gently. Place crumb side up, on greased baking sheet; sprinkle with grated Parmesan cheese. Bake for 12 to 14 minutes or till golden. Serve warm.

CRÈME BRÛLÉE WITH STRAWBERRIES
Serves 6
Unbelievably delicious, with or without strawberries!

2 cups heavy cream	4 tablespoons white sugar
½ inch vanilla bean or 1 table-	½ cup light brown sugar
spoon vanilla	3 cups strawberries, washed and
2 eggs	hulled (optional)
2 egg yolks	

1. Heat cream with vanilla bean or vanilla in heavy saucepan over low heat. Beat eggs and yolks adding white sugar gradually; beat until light and thick. Slowly pour cream into egg mixture, mixing well.

2. Return mixture to heavy sauce pan and cook on low heat, stirring with wooden spoon until mixture coats back of spoon. Do not boil. Remove vanilla bean.

3. Pour into shallow 1½ quart casserole or individual porcelain ramekins (ovenproof), and cool to room temperature. Cover with plastic wrap and refrigerate overnight.

4. At serving time, sieve brown sugar over top, covering custard completely (to about ¼-inch thickness). Place casserole in pan of crushed ice and place under hot broiler until sugar melts and caramelizes. This may take less than a minute, so watch constantly.

5. Chill about 5 minutes in refrigerator to harden sugar crust. To serve, crack crust with back of serving spoon and spoon over bowls of chilled strawberries.

VARIATION:

POACHED PEARS WITH CRÈME BRÛLÉE

6 medium winter pears	¼ cup lemon juice
1⅓ cups sugar	

1. Pare pears, leaving stems on. In 5-quart saucepan, mix 2 cups of water with sugar and lemon juice. Bring to boil, stirring to dissolve sugar.

2. Place pears on their side in syrup. Simmer, covered, 15

minutes. Turn pears, simmer, uncovered for 15 minutes longer. Refrigerate overnight in syrup.

3. To serve, place pears in individual serving dishes. At table, spoon Crème Brûlée over top of pears.

Let's Pull Together

Polynesian Meatballs
Rice Pilaf with Vermicelli
Lettuce Salad
Chocolate Mocha Tortes

POLYNESIAN MEATBALLS
Serves 6
Can also be used as a great appetizer!

1½ pounds ground beef
1½ teaspoons salt
¼ teaspoon pepper
1 egg, slightly beaten
1 2¼-ounce can of deviled ham (optional)
⅓ cup soy sauce
3 tablespoons cornstarch
½ cup chopped celery
¼ cup chopped onion
1 10½-ounce can chicken broth, undiluted
½ cup cider vinegar
⅓ cup light corn syrup
2 tablespoons light brown sugar
2 large green peppers, cut in thin strips
2 red peppers, cut in thin strips (optional)
2 8¼-ounce cans pineapple chunks, drained
1 8-ounce can sliced water chestnuts, drained
8 maraschino cherries or 1 large tomato cut in wedges

1. Early in day, mix beef, salt, pepper, egg, and ham (if desired) together and form into 16 balls. Broil meatballs on rimmed cookie sheet until brown, shaking sheet occasionally, so meatballs cook evenly all over. Remove from broiler and set aside.

2. Combine ⅓ cup of soy sauce and cornstarch. Set aside. In the drippings from meatballs, sauté in large skillet the celery and onion until onion is golden. Stir in chicken broth, vinegar, corn syrup, and sugar. Stir in soy sauce and cornstarch mixture.

3. Cook at medium heat stirring constantly until thick and transparent. Add meatballs and rest of ingredients. Cook over low heat 10 minutes. Serve.

RICE PILAF WITH VERMICELLI
Serves 6

3 tablespoons butter
1 cup long-grain regular or converted rice
½ cup thin spaghetti broken into small pieces

2 cups boiling chicken or beef broth
Salt (optional)
¼ teaspoon pepper

1. In heavy, 2-quart saucepan melt butter over moderate heat and brown broken spaghetti. Add rice and cook 2 to 3 minutes, stirring often, until grains are hot and shiny.
2. Add broth carefully to rice and bring to boil. Add pepper. Reduce heat to low, cover pan, and cook 20 minutes, until rice is tender and liquid in pan is absorbed.

LETTUCE SALAD
Serves 4

1 medium head of lettuce
1 tablespoon wine vinegar
2 teaspoons Dijon mustard
1 shallot, chopped fine
2 tablespoons heavy cream
½ teaspoon salt

Freshly ground pepper
2 tablespoons salad oil
1 clove garlic, crushed
¼ cup chopped walnuts
2 tablespoons chopped parsley

1. Wash lettuce, and tear into bite-sized pieces. Dry with paper towels. Mix vinegar, mustard, shallot, cream, salt, pepper, and garlic in bowl. Whisk in oil.
2. Toss lettuce with dressing. Sprinkle with walnuts and parsley. Toss again and serve immediately.

CHOCOLATE MOCHA TORTES
Makes 24

2 5.3-ounce cans evaporated milk

4 squares unsweetened chocolate

1 cup sugar

2 tablespoons butter

½ cup butter, melted

1 box Nabisco Famous Chocolate Wafers, crushed

½ gallon coffee or peppermint ice cream, softened

Whipped cream

Chopped nuts

Maraschino cherries

1. Combine milk, chocolate, sugar, and 2 tablespoons butter, and cook until thick. Cool until almost cold.

2. Mix chocolate wafers and ½ cup butter to make a crust. Press crust into 24 cupcake papers in muffin tin. Spoon ice cream into cupcake papers, making each about ⅔ full. Place in freezer until ice cream hardens.

3. Top each cupcake with cooled chocolate sauce. Cover with plastic wrap and freeze.

4. To serve, set out about 10 minutes before serving. Top with whipped cream, chopped nuts, and a cherry.

5
Time for Romance

Caring and Craving
Paradise Found
You Tiger, You!
Sizzle and Spice

Supper Warm-up

One night late, or rather early, about three in the morning, I awakened feeling very amorous. I snuggled up to Charlie and kissed him tenderly while he slept.

He never woke up, but only mumbled happily, "Who is it?" and then rolled over away from me.

I recoiled in utter dismay. *Who is it?,* I thought to myself. *What does he mean, "*Who is it?*" Who does he think it is? Who else could it be?*

I never mentioned the episode to Charlie the next morning. I was terribly afraid that the "somebody else" who was lurking in his dream world might become *conscious.* The horrible thought occurred to me that maybe Charlie's dream was more exciting than his reality. I decided I'd better spice up reality.

That morning was Monday, a very blue Monday. As Charlie left for the office, I somehow knew it was going to be one of those days. He paused reluctantly at the front door, and I gave him a little verbal shove to get him going.

We were in the proverbial rut. After six years of marriage and two active little girls, our moonlight and roses had turned to daylight and dishes. And Mondays, blue Mondays! *All* our days felt like blue Mondays.

That morning I determined to make Charlie's homecoming that evening extraspecial. I bought a roast and scurried around the kitchen preparing a fancy dinner. At 4:30, I took a bubble bath, and then, on a whim, put on pink baby-doll pajamas and white boots to greet him at the front door.

Weary from the chariot race home on the expressway, my unsuspecting husband took one look at me and lost his balance on the front step.

But he must have liked what he saw. That night the Morgan household was transformed from Dullsville to Funsville—blue to red. The beginnings of romance.

Of course, it's not always possible to keep up that pace every day. I mean, who looks romantic mopping up spilled milk, scraping eggs off the dishes, and dodging skateboards?

And what about the kids? They're another story and another

problem. Unfortunately, our nights of total romance are fewer and farther between as Laura and Michelle grow up. I find that I can't entertain romantic ideas with their curious eyes wide open. So my night of fun usually begins when theirs is over.

Romantic dinners for lovers are one of the sweet pleasures of life, and if you don't initiate one, who will? Remember the thrill of that special dinner before you were married? Whether it's three or twenty-three years later, it can even be better than ever. A late intimate dinner for two beside a crackling fire, or on the back porch amid balmy breezes will help set the atmosphere.

The setting and your attitude are as important as the food. Romance means giving him space to relax. Romance is freedom, the unexpected, the pleasant touch of beauty.

A husband will usually respond when the table is lighted with candles, living flowers, and colors that rev up his senses. No matter how long he's been married, he wants to linger with his woman who is exciting and inviting. *This woman can be you.*

These menus are designed to help grab your husband's attention. Once you have it, the rest is up to you. The dinner may have to wait.

Caring and Craving

VEAL FRANÇAIS
Serves 2
A beautiful, quick main dish.

½ pound thin veal scallops, pounded (ask your butcher to do this for you)
¼ cup flour, spread in a saucer
1 tablespoon olive or salad oil
2 tablespoons butter
1 tablespoon lemon juice
2 tablespoons chicken broth
1 tablespoon chopped parsley
1 lemon, thinly sliced
¼ teaspoon caraway seeds (optional)

1. Flour scallops on one side only. Heat 1 tablespoon oil and 2 tablespoons butter until quite hot. Sauté scallops on floured side first for about 2 minutes. The oil should be hot enough to make the meat sizzle. Turn and sauté 2 minutes more. Shake skillet occasionally during cooking and don't crowd scallops in pan. When done, remove from skillet to heated platter. Season with salt and pepper. You may need more oil and butter for remaining scallops.

2. After all scallops are cooked, remove skillet from heat and add 1 tablespoon butter, 2 tablespoons chicken broth and lemon juice, stirring to loosen pan juices. Pour over scallops, sprinkle with parsley, garnish with lemon slices and caraway seeds, and serve immediately.

VARIATION: Chicken scallops may be substituted for veal; a lot less expensive, and the taste is still terrific.

ROMAINE SALAD
Serves 2

½ head romaine lettuce
4 tablespoons red wine vinegar
¼ cup oil
½ teaspoon sugar
1 egg yolk
¼ teaspoon dry mustard
¼ teaspoon salt

2 tablespoons chopped parsley
Salt, pepper, and garlic powder
    to taste
Croutons (optional)
A few macadamia nuts, chopped
    (optional)

1. Put in blender or whisk in small bowl red-wine vinegar, oil, sugar, egg yolk, and spices. For best results, make dressing a day ahead to allow the full flavor of the ingredients to blend.

2. When ready to eat, break romaine into bite size pieces, toss lightly with desired amount of dressing, and serve with croutons and nuts.

TIP: Bring store-bought croutons to life by sprinkling melted butter and garlic salt over them and baking for 10 minutes in 350° oven.

FANTASY RICE
Serves 2

¼ cup raw converted rice
⅛ teaspoon salt
¼ can chicken broth plus enough
    water to equal ½ cup
1 teaspoon butter

1 tablespoon chopped green
    onions (optional)
2 tablespoons macadamia nuts,
    chopped

Mix rice, salt, and chicken liquid in saucepan. Bring to a boil, stir once or twice. Lower heat, cover pan and simmer 14 minutes without stirring or until all liquid is absorbed. Let set covered a few minutes off heat. (In any recipe, if rice doesn't absorb liquid after 15 minutes, simply drain.) Stir in onions, butter and nuts. Sprinkle with chopped parsley, if desired.

BOUDOIR CHEESE CAKE
Serves 8

1 9-inch baked graham-cracker crust
3 3-ounce packages cream cheese
1 cup sugar
Dash of salt
2 teaspoons lemon juice
2 eggs, separated
1 teaspoon vanilla
Dash of nutmeg (optional)
1 cup heavy cream, whipped

1. Beat together cream cheese, sugar, and salt. Beat egg yolks; add to cheese mixture.

2. Beat egg whites until stiff and fold into cheese mixture. Fold in whipped cream and vanilla. Pour into pie crust. Freeze. Cover with plastic wrap.

Paradise Found

Chicken Parmesan
Green-Chili Rice
Tomatoes Provençal
Chocolate-Bar Angel Pie

CHICKEN PARMESAN
Serves 2
Juicy and crusty.

1 3-pound frying chicken, cut up
6 tablespoons butter, melted
3 tablespoons bread crumbs
½ cup grated Parmesan cheese
Dash of garlic salt
Dash of paprika
¼ cup chopped parsley (optional)

1. Dip chicken pieces in butter. Shake remaining ingredients in paper bag; add chicken and shake until coated.
2. Butter a 9 x 13-inch baking dish; add chicken pieces. Bake at 350° for 1½ hours.

GREEN-CHILI RICE
Serves 2
Prepare this early in the day. Double the recipe and freeze half for another romantic night.

¼ cup plus 2 tablespoons raw rice
½ cup sour cream
⅛ teaspoon salt
Few dashes of pepper
3 ounces Monterey Jack cheese, cut in strips
½ of 3-ounce can jalapeño peppers seeds removed, chopped
¼ cup grated Monterey Jack cheese

1. Preheat oven to 350°. Cook and drain rice. Add sour cream, and salt and pepper to taste.

2. Arrange half of rice mixture in greased casserole, top with strips of cheese, then sprinkle on all chopped peppers.

3. Add remaining rice mixture, cover with grated cheese and bake in oven for 30 minutes.

TOMATOES PROVENÇAL
Serves 2

2 tomatoes	2 finely chopped tarragon leaves
Salt	2 teaspoons chopped parsley
Freshly ground black pepper	3 tablespoons olive oil
4 finely chopped shallots or	1 tablespoon wine vinegar
scallions	Salt and pepper to taste
2 finely chopped basil leaves	1 teaspoon Dijon mustard

1. Wash tomatoes and cut off top ⅓ horizontally; discard tops. Arrange tomatoes, cut side up, on serving dish; season generously with salt and ground black pepper.

2. Sprinkle each tomato half thickly with finely chopped shallots or scallions. Mix the fresh herbs together and sprinkle each tomato half with a thick green layer of freshly chopped herbs.

3. Mix oil and rest of ingredients and drizzle 2 to 3 tablespoons on each tomato half.

CHOCOLATE-BAR ANGEL PIE
Serves 6–8

3 egg whites	Pinch of salt
¼ teaspoon cream of tartar	1 cup sugar

Beat whites, cream of tartar, and salt until frothy. Add sugar, beating until stiff. Spread in well-buttered 8 or 9-inch pie pan, building up sides. Bake 1 hour at 275°.

FILLING

1½ cups miniature or 15 large
   marshmallows
½ cup milk
1½ cups heavy cream, whipped,
   or 1 13.5-ounce carton of
   Cool Whip

1 teaspoon vanilla
1 8-ounce Hershey candy bar
   with almonds
2 teaspoons instant coffee
   powder

1. In top of double boiler, melt marshmallows in milk over simmering water. Add broken candy bar pieces and stir until melted. Add coffee powder. Stir in vanilla and cool.

2. Fold in whipped cream or Cool Whip. Pour into meringue and chill for 24 hours.

VARIATION: In place of meringue shell, use 1⅓ cups flaked coconut mixed with 2 teaspoons butter. Press into 8- or 9-inch pie pan. Bake at 325° for 15 minutes. Pour filling into crust and chill.

You Tiger, You!

ROAST PORK TENDERLOIN
Serves 2
Leftovers make delicious sandwiches.

4 slices bacon
1 pound whole pork tenderloin

1 tablespoon Dijon mustard
Salt and pepper

1. Partially cook bacon; drain on paper toweling. Fold under tip of tenderloin to form 5- to 6-inch long roast. Spread roast with mustard; sprinkle with little salt and pepper.

2. Wrap bacon slices around meat roll; tie roast securely. Place pork on rack in shallow roasting pan. Roast, uncovered, in 325° oven for 1 to 1¼ hours until meat thermometer registers 170°.

EASY STUFFED POTATOES
Serves 2

2 large baking potatoes
¼ cup salad dressing
¼ cup milk

Salt
Pepper
Parsley (optional)

Bake potatoes at 400° for one hour. Cut off tops; scoop out pulp and mash with salad dressing, milk, salt, and pepper. Restuff potatoes. Sprinkle with parsley if desired.

CARROTS GLACÉ
Serves 4–6

4 medium-sized carrots
2 teaspoons butter
1 tablespoon dark corn syrup
1 teaspoon brown sugar

½ teaspoon freshly grated orange rind or dash of nutmeg
2 teaspoons toasted slivered almonds

1. Cut carrots in half lengthwise or in diagonal 1-inch slices. Boil in covered skillet in small amount of salted water, just to cover carrots, about 10 minutes. Remove cover and boil 5 more minutes. Water may boil away, so be careful not to burn carrots. When tender, drain off any remaining water.

2. To skillet, add butter, syrup, brown sugar, orange rind and almonds. Shake carrots to coat with glaze and simmer in mixture 5 more minutes, shaking pan occasionally.

ONION HERB BREAD

1 small loaf French bread
¼ cup butter, melted
1 teaspoon snipped parsley
¼ teaspoon salt

Dash of onion salt
Dash of thyme
Pinch of cayenne pepper
Dash of paprika

1. Cut bread in ½-inch slices, leaving bottom crust intact. Set aside on piece of foil large enough to wrap bread.

2. Stir spices into butter. Spread between bread slices. Bring sides of foil up over top of loaf. Twist ends to close loosely. Bake at 425° 10 minutes or until bread is warm.

GOLDEN PINEAPPLE ICE-CREAM SUNDAES
Serves 2

Vanilla ice cream
1 tablespoon butter
1½ tablespoons brown sugar
1½ teaspoons lemon juice

½ cup fresh or canned pineapple chunks
¼ cup slivered almonds or macadamia nuts (optional)

1. Preheat oven to 350°. Toast almonds or macadamia nuts on cookie sheet in oven for about 5 minutes. Watch so they don't burn. Set aside in little bowl to cool.

2. Melt butter in small pan; add sugar and stir over heat until bubbly. Stir in lemon juice.

3. Put pineapple in small baking dish. Pour sugar mixture over top. Bake 14 minutes stirring once or twice.

4. Scoop vanilla ice cream into dessert dishes. Top with spoonfuls of hot pineapple topping and sprinkling of nuts.

Sizzle and Spice

Marinated Flank Steak
Oven-browned Potato Fans
Sautéed Mushrooms
Spinach in Cream
Chocolate Cream Pie

MARINATED FLANK STEAK
Serves 2

1½-pounds flank steak   ⅓ cup French Dressing (low cal-
                                     orie dressing may be used)

Brush both sides of steak with dressing, and refrigerate in dish for several hours. Grill or broil a few minutes on each side, and slice diagonally against the grain. Delicious!

OVEN-BROWNED POTATO FANS
Serves 2

2 medium baking potatoes   Freshly ground pepper
2 tablespoons melted butter   Paprika
Seasoned salt   Chopped parsley (garnish)

1. Preheat oven to 400°. Peel potatoes and remove small slice from bottom so potato will sit on flat surface. Keep in cold water to prevent darkening.
2. Insert skewer lengthwise into potato ¾ inch from bottom. Beginning ½ inch from end of potato, slice down to skewer every ⅛ inch. Potato is to remain in one piece. Carefully remove skewer and place back in cold water.
3. When potatoes are ready, pat dry on paper towels and place in shallow, oiled baking dish. Baste fan shapes with melted butter

and sprinkle with seasoned salt. Bake 45 minutes. This may be done several hours ahead.

4. Twenty minutes before dinner, baste again with melted butter; sprinkle with paprika and bake 15 to 20 minutes until golden brown. To serve, sprinkle parsley over top.

SAUTÉED MUSHROOMS
Serves 2

½ pound mushrooms, wiped clean with wet paper towel
2 tablespoons butter
2 teaspoons fresh lemon juice

¼ teaspoon salt
Chopped parsley (optional)
Cayenne pepper (optional)

1. Cut off mushroom stems (save stems for another purpose). With small sharp knife, cut grooves on each mushroom that spiral out from center to edges.

2. Heat butter in skillet, add mushrooms, fluted side down, veins up. Add salt and lemon juice; cook gently for 4 to 5 minutes, then turn over and cook briefly. Sprinkle with parsley and a dash of cayenne pepper. Serve immediately.

SPINACH IN CREAM
Serves 2

1 package frozen spinach, thawed, drained, and uncooked
2 tablespoons butter

3 green onions, chopped
½ teaspoon nutmeg
3 tablespoons milk or cream

Melt butter, add onions, nutmeg, and cream. Add spinach. Heat through.

CHOCOLATE CREAM PIE

1 9-inch baked pastry shell or   ½ teaspoon cinnamon
   crumb crust   2¾ cups milk
½ cup cocoa   2 tablespoons butter
1¼ cups sugar   1 tablespoon vanilla
¼ cup cornstarch   ½ cup heavy cream, whipped
¼ teaspoon salt   2 teaspoons sugar

1. Combine cocoa, sugar, salt, and cornstarch in a medium saucepan. Gradually blend milk into dry ingredients, stirring until smooth. Cook over medium heat, stirring constantly, until mixture boils; boil one minute.

2. Remove from heat; blend in butter, vanilla, and cinnamon. Cool slightly. Pour into pie crust. Carefully press plastic wrap directly onto pie filling. Chill 3 to 4 hours.

3. Whip cream and 2 teaspoons sugar in small chilled bowl. Top each piece of pie with dollop of whipped cream.

6
Ho-Hum Tuesdays

Everybody's Favorite
Country Classic
Happy Days
Engine Starter

Salads, Sex, and Fish Sticks

Today is Tuesday, a ho-hum Tuesday.

It's not a holiday. It isn't anybody's birthday. Nobody graduated. No one is coming for dinner. It will just be us, the four of us.

Next Sunday is Mimi's birthday. Charlie's grandmother will be 88 years old, and I'm planning a party for twenty of her closest friends. I have decided on the menu and have begun to shop for food.

Last night I baked and froze two party cakes. On Saturday, Charlie will help me rearrange the furniture and set up borrowed tables. By Sunday, I don't think I'll recognize my own house. I love parties.

So here I sit, planning and preparing for a week ahead, for one meal that will probably be eaten and over in less than an hour. And in the meantime, my family will be the losers.

Like last night. I had just started to frost a birthday cake when the littlest Morgan appeared at my side.

"Um, Mommy," she said with a snuggle. "That smells good."

I had heard that line before, but was determined not to weaken.

"Not this one, Honey," I told her, "but here's a beater to lick," knowing in my heart that it would never suffice.

At that instant, Laura came from nowhere to reach for the other beater. Where she had been waiting until that moment, I'll never know. But her timing was split second.

Within ten seconds, in came Charlie. He, too, had been tempted by the smell of freshly baked cake, and I saw him eyeing my work of art.

"Who's that looking in the window?" he asked. I turned quickly, but then remembered Charlie's age-old trick of diversion. As I looked back around, I saw his finger reaching for the icing.

"Don't you dare!" I scolded. "That's for Mimi's party. Don't touch, any of you."

I thought later, *Here I am baking cakes for outsiders, but my own family can't touch them 'til Sunday. It really doesn't seem fair.*

Which brings us back to Tuesday. Ho-hum Tuesday. An ordinary, humdrum day. *What'll we eat tonight? We could bring in hamburgers, but that was last night. I just don't have time for tonight's dinner.*

When ho-hum Tuesdays become ho-hum Wednesdays and ho-hum Thursdays, there's a danger that entire weeks may become ho-hummers. Day-in and day-out living can swiftly slip into tedious sameness.

But, it's really so *easy* to make Tuesday a little bit special. And Wednesday. Or any other day.

Variety is the spice of sex. And salads. And chicken.

Jazz up the hamburgers. Wrap fried fish sticks in newspaper, English-Pub-style. Spread open a Boston lettuce, and tuck daisies in between the leaves for a perky centerpiece. Spice up the tea. Color menus for each place setting. Use good china. Use shock value. Dazzle their eyeballs, *jar* them from their lethargy. Eat outside, or *under* the dining room table!

Tuesday night. *Let's see. Maybe I'll try some pink food coloring in the mashed potatoes. . . .*

Everybody's Favorite

> *Burger Surprise*
> *Oven French Fries*
> *Broccoli Supreme*
> *Lettuce Wedges with Russian Dressing*
> *Krazy Kake with Quick Chocolate Icing*

BURGER SURPRISE
Serves 6

2 pounds ground beef
1 cup finely diced celery
2 tablespoons butter
1 egg beaten
1½ teaspoons salt
¼ teaspoon pepper

½ cup water
2 teaspoons Worcestershire sauce
2 tablespoons chopped parsley
¼ cup chopped slivered almonds
6 English muffins, split

1. Sauté celery in butter until soft. In large bowl mix celery with remaining ingredients. Shape into 6 large patties.

2. Fry patties in 2 teaspoons hot butter in large frying pan, about 3 minutes on each side, or broil on charcoal grill.

3. Serve on buttered, toasted English-muffin halves. Top each burger with spoonful of chili sauce.

OVEN FRENCH FRIES
Serves 6

3 Idaho baking potatoes
1 tablespoon vegetable oil
1 tablespoon butter, melted

Paprika
Salt

1. Preheat oven to 450°. Scrub potatoes, but do not pare. Cut in half lengthwise; cut each half into 8 lengthwise strips, leaving on peel. Soak strips in bowl of cold water for 20 minutes.

2. Blot potato strips dry on paper toweling; place in a small bowl. Sprinkle with oil, butter and paprika and stir well to coat evenly. Arrange strips in single layer on cookie sheet.

3. Bake for 20 minutes, stirring frequently to brown evenly. Potatoes are cooked when crisp and golden outside and tender when tested with fork. Blot well on paper toweling; sprinkle with salt.

BROCCOLI SUPREME
Serves 4
Sensational. Even the kids love it!

1 tablespoon butter	**1 10-ounce package frozen, chopped broccoli, cooked and drained**
1 small onion, chopped	
1 clove garlic, minced (optional)	
¾ cup chopped mushrooms or celery	**½ can mushroom soup, undiluted**
	¼ pound Cheddar cheese, grated
½ cup slivered almonds	**⅓ cup commercial sour cream**

1. Sauté onions, garlic, mushrooms, and almonds in butter until lightly browned. Can be done early in day.

2. Mix soup, cheese, and sour cream with mushroom mixture and broccoli. Pour into baking dish. Bake 20 minutes at 350°.

NOTE: Drained asparagus or cooked chopped cauliflower may be used as substitute for broccoli. *Any* combination of vegetables is good. For a different touch add French fried onion rings to casserole, reserving a few to sprinkle on top.

For a quicker version, simply mix together in baking dish 1 10-ounce package frozen broccoli, cooked and drained, ½ can mushroom soup, and ¼ cup sour cream. Sprinkle with 3 tablespoons of grated Parmesan cheese and 2 tablespoons of melted butter. Bake 30 minutes at 350°.

LETTUCE WEDGES WITH RUSSIAN DRESSING
Serves 6

1 small head lettuce, cut into 6   ⅓ cup chili sauce
   wedges   2 tablespoons milk
½ cup mayonnaise   1 tablespoon sweet relish

Chill lettuce wedges in plastic bag in refrigerator. Mix remaining ingredients together; cover and chill. At serving time, spoon dressing over wedges on salad plates.

KRAZY KAKE
Makes 9 squares

1 cup sugar   2 teaspoons vanilla
1½ cups flour   ½ cup oil
⅓ cup cocoa   1 cup cold water
1 teaspoon baking soda   2 tablespoons vinegar
½ teaspoon salt

1. Preheat oven to 375°. Butter an 8-inch square or a 9-inch round cake pan. Measure all ingredients, except vinegar, into pan. Stir them well with fork or wire whisk until thoroughly blended.

2. Add vinegar and stir quickly to thoroughly blend in, and immediately place in oven. There must be no delay in baking after vinegar is added. Bake cake for 20 to 25 minutes or until center is slightly puffed and sides begin to pull away from pan. Cool. Sprinkle top with powdered sugar before serving or spread with icing.

QUICK CHOCOLATE ICING

1 cup semisweet chocolate chips   ¼ cup strong coffee

Melt chocolate chips in coffee. Beat until creamy and spread on cake.

Country Classic

SWEET 'N SOUR BEANS AND FRANKS
Serves 6–8

4 slices bacon
¼ cup chopped green pepper
¼ cup chopped onion
½ pound frankfurters, whole or sliced into 1-inch pieces
2 16-ounce cans baked beans in tomato sauce
1 8½-ounce can pineapple tidbits, drained

2 teaspoons prepared mustard
½ cup catsup
3 tablespoons brown sugar
1 tablespoon Worcestershire sauce
½ envelope dry onion soup mix (optional)
2 tablespoons corn syrup or molasses

1. Preheat oven to 350°. Fry bacon in skillet until crisp. Drain on paper towels and crumble. In 2 tablespoons bacon drippings, sauté pepper and onion 3 minutes until tender. Stir in rest of ingredients and bacon; mix well.

2. Bake in 2-quart casserole, uncovered 1 hour. Stir occasionally during baking. This may be prepared early in day and baked at dinnertime.

SALLY LUNN BREAD
Easy, sweet bread

2 cups flour
3 teaspoons baking powder
½ teaspoon salt
½ cup butter

1 cup sugar
2 eggs
1 cup milk

1. Preheat oven to 375°. Sift flour, baking powder, and salt together. Set aside.

2. Beat butter and sugar together until creamy; add eggs and beat well. Stir dry ingredients into butter mixture, alternately with milk.

3. Bake in a buttered 9 x 5-inch loaf pan for 40 to 50 minutes. Serve warm or cold with apple butter. Tastes good the next morning toasted with butter and cinnamon sugar.

(When I was single, my friend Sandy Buell often shared this yummy bread with me. Her husband, Jon, was one of the happiest husbands I had ever seen. I made a mental note to make this in *my* home someday!)

HARVEST JELL-O SALAD
Serves 4

1 3-ounce package orange
  gelatin
2 cups apple cider or apple juice

1 tablespoon lemon juice
1 apple, cored and cubed
¼ cup chopped nuts

1. Dissolve gelatin in 1 cup boiling apple cider. Add second cup of cold cider and lemon juice. Chill until mixture is thick as unbeaten egg whites.

2. Add apples and walnuts to gelatin. Pour into pretty mold and chill until firm. Unmold and serve on small cake stand or pretty plate.

YOGURT POPSICLES
Makes 6 popsicles

**1 3-ounce package any flavor   1 8-ounce container vanilla
   gelatin   yogurt
1 cup boiling water   1½ tablespoons honey**

1. Dissolve gelatin in boiling water. Chill until slightly thickened. Beat in yogurt and honey until smooth and combined, about 1 minute. Pour mixture into 3½-ounce paper drinking cups. Freeze.

2. Insert wooden skewers or rolled paper lollipop sticks when pops are partially frozen. Tear off paper cups before serving.

Happy Days

Shapely Meatloaf
Technicolorful Mashed Potatoes
Herbed Corn on the Cob
English Cheese Muffins
Raspberry Jam Peaches

SHAPELY MEATLOAF
Serves 6–8

1½ pounds ground beef
½ cup cracker crumbs
1 beaten egg
¼ teaspoon dried thyme
1 10-ounce can onion soup, undiluted
¼ cup finely chopped onion

2 tablespoons chopped green pepper or shredded carrot
1 tablespoon steak sauce
2 teaspoons Worcestershire sauce
½ teaspoon salt
¼ teaspoon pepper

1. Preheat oven to 350°. Combine all ingredients. Shape this mixture into mold approximately two inches deep. Instead of the typical pan, use an unusual mold, like a fish-shaped mold or ring mold.

2. Bake about 1¼ hours. Let meatloaf sit in pan for 10 minutes before you unmold it. It will be firmer and easier to slice.

VARIATION:

BARBECUE-SAUCED MEAT LOAF

½ cup tomato sauce
⅓ cup water
3 tablespoons brown sugar
3 tablespoons vinegar

Dash of Tabasco sauce
2 tablespoons prepared mustard
2 teaspoons Worcestershire sauce

Combine all ingredients; pour over meat loaf. Bake at 350° for 1 hour and 15 minutes, basting occasionally with sauce.

TECHNICOLORFUL MASHED POTATOES

5 potatoes
½ cup hot milk, or cream (if you're skinny)
Food coloring (any color)
1 beaten egg

2 tablespoons butter
Salt and pepper
Dash of freshly ground nutmeg (optional)

1. Peel potatoes; cook in boiling, salted water until tender.
2. Drain and place potatoes back in cooking pot, shaking over low heat to dry.
3. Using potato masher or electric mixer at low speed, add egg and hot milk as needed and continue beating until light and fluffy. During this process add your favorite food color to create desired results (I suggest pink). Add salt, pepper, and butter as desired.

TIP: Instead of boiling potatoes and going through all that peeling (ugh!), simply bake potatoes in 350° oven for one hour. Scoop out pulp and whip according to instructions above. You can pile potatoes back into the skins, if you like. Decorate with tiny flags, Japanese umbrellas, or anything that's handy.

HERBED CORN ON THE COB

1 ear of corn for each person
½ cup milk
½ cup butter, softened

½ teaspoon crushed marjoram
½ teaspoon dried crushed rosemary

1. Cook fresh corn in small amount of salted water (just enough to cover) and ½ cup milk for about 6 to 8 minutes. Or use frozen corn on the cob, cooking as directed.
2. Add marjoram and rosemary to butter, blend with spoon until fluffy. Slather on hot corn.

CHEESE ENGLISH MUFFINS

4 English muffins, split
1 10-ounce package Cheddar
   cheese, grated
½ cup butter

½ cup chopped green onions
¼ cup chopped parsley
2 tablespoons lemon juice

Lightly butter and toast English muffins. Mix rest of ingredients together and spread on muffin halves. Bake on cookie sheet in 400° oven for 10 minutes.

RASPBERRY JAM PEACHES
Serves 6

3 ripe but firm peaches
6 teaspoons raspberry jam

3 macaroon cookies or vanilla
   wafers, crumbled

Peel and cut peaches in half. Place in buttered pie plate or baking dish. Put spoonful of raspberry jam in center of each peach half, and sprinkle with cookie crumbs. Bake at 350° for 10 minutes. Turn off oven and let sit in oven until dessert time.

Engine Starter

APRICOT-GLAZED BAKED CHICKEN
Serves 8

2 3-pound fryers, cut into serving
pieces
1 8-ounce bottle Russian salad
dressing
1 8-ounce bottle apricot
preserves

1 envelope onion soup mix
Watercress (optional)
1 bunch green grapes (optional)

1. Mix dressing, preserves, and soup mix in small pan. Bring to boil, cool slightly. Pour over chicken in shallow baking dish. Marinate for several hours.

2. Bake at 350° for 1 hour, or at 325° for 1¼ hours. Serve on bed of watercress and garnish platter with green grapes.

TIP: The apricot glaze is also great on chops, hamburgers, and spareribs.

VARIATION: One 8-ounce bottle of French dressing and one 12-ounce can whole cranberries may be substituted for Russian dressing and apricot preserves.

DEEP-FRIED POTATO PUFFS
Serves 8

3 pounds firm baking potatoes, baked and scooped out
¼ cup heavy cream
¼ cup butter
1 teaspoon salt
2 egg yolks
1 cup water
6 tablespoons unsalted butter, cut into ½-inch bits

¼ teaspoon salt
1 cup all-purpose flour
4 eggs
Freshly grated nutmeg
Vegetable oil or shortening for deep-frying

1. Mix potato pulp with cream, ¼ cup butter, 1 teaspoon salt and 2 egg yolks. Mash well.

2. In saucepan, heat water, butter bits, ¼ teaspoon salt until mixture boils rapidly. Add flour, remove from heat, and beat in quickly. Hold pan above heat and beat vigorously until dough is thick and forms into a ball. Do not overbeat.

3. Add eggs, one at a time, beating well after each addition. Beat mashed potatoes thoroughly into mixture and correct the seasoning. At this stage potato mixture can safely be covered and kept at room temperature for 2 to 3 hours. Pour oil into deep fryer or large, heavy saucepan to depth of at least 3 inches and heat until oil reaches temperature of 370°.

4. Shape mixture into balls and deep fry (370°) until lightly browned and puffed. Drain on paper towels and keep warm on paper-lined cookie sheet in low oven until all are fried. Serve hot.

OLD-FASHIONED STRAWBERRY JAM

1 quart sweet strawberries
2 cups sugar, divided
1 tablespoon cornstarch

Dash of cinnamon
Dash of cloves
Dash of mace

1. Wash berries, remove stems and dry berries on paper towel. Stir berries and 1¾ cup sugar together in large sauce pan and cook

slowly over medium heat for 10 minutes, or until juice has thickened slightly. Do not stir while cooking.

2. Combine cornstarch with remaining ¼ cup sugar and spices, and blend into small amount of hot strawberry syrup. When mixed, stir into berry mixture in pan and cook, stirring constantly, 3 more minutes. Jam will not be as thick as commercial jams, but much more delicious.

3. Serve with slice of your favorite French bread.

CHEESE-BAKED CELERY
Serves 6–8

4 cups thinly sliced celery	**2 tablespoons chopped green**
¼ cup melted butter	**pepper or onion, or both**
3 tablespoons flour	**2 tablespoons chopped pimento**
1 teaspoon salt	**1 cup shredded sharp Cheddar**
1 cup milk	**cheese**
1 4-ounce can chopped mush-	**1 cup of soft bread crumbs**
rooms, drained	**2 tablespoons melted butter**

1. Sauté celery in ¼ cup melted butter in a large skillet until crisp but tender, about 5 minutes. Push celery to one side, and stir in flour and salt; stir until smooth. Add milk, stirring until well blended; cook until mixture is smooth and thickened, about 5 minutes, stirring constantly.

2. Add mushrooms, green pepper, and/or onion, pimento, and cheese to celery mixture; stir until cheese is melted.

3. Spoon mixture into greased 2-quart shallow casserole. Combine bread crumbs and 2 tablespoons melted butter; toss well, and sprinkle over celery mixture. Bake at 350° for 20 minutes.

GREEN GRAPES WITH GINGER CREAM
Serves 6

3 cups green seedless grapes, washed and dried on paper towels
1½ cups sour cream
1½ teaspoons vanilla or 1 teaspoon lime juice

4 tablespoons brown sugar
2 teaspoons crystalized ginger, chopped finely or ½ teaspoon ground ginger

1. Lightly toss grapes with sour cream and vanilla or lime juice to coat. Refrigerate.

2. Mix sugar and ginger and set aside. When ready to serve, spoon grapes into dessert dishes or small melon halves. Sprinkle with sugar mixture. Easy and lovely.

VARIATION: Substitute 1 cup yogurt in place of sour cream and sweeten with 2 tablespoons honey instead of brown sugar.

7
For Men Only

The Gang's All Here
Halftime Show
Uh-Oh-Overtime
Victory Party

A Housewife's Guide to Coping
with Football Season

My husband is a football fan. No, make that a *nut*. That means on
any Sunday afternoon from August through January, he can be
found either in front of the TV or at the stadium, in a dazed, semi-
conscious condition.

I have made one important discovery. The wife of a football fan is
herself either a football fan or a football widow.

I must admit that I've become an avid fan of the Miami Dolphins,
and I really enjoy those games. But when other teams are playing on
TV, I'm simply not a purist. I can't enjoy a football game just because it's a football game.

For one thing, I can't understand all those interruptions during a
game. Why do twenty-two players spend several seconds running
around and then all get together and talk about it for several more
minutes?

When the Miami Dolphins aren't playing on TV, I excuse myself
and leave Charlie alone. I am sure he doesn't even miss me until he's
hungry.

On football Sundays, I scrap all plans for family mealtimes. I
know that the game (or games) may run from three to six hours.
Charlie, therefore, won't be joining the rest of the family for any
traditional meal, but he'll want to eat *during* the game—all the
games—rather like being served at a continuous cafeteria.

One Sunday afternoon I decided to figure out how to handle this
weekly problem. I needed a strategy to keep my children occupied
and my husband supplied with food and drink, and still use those
hours for my own advantage. I went to the TV room and came up
with *my* game plan.

First of all, I saw there were distinct time periods, which helped
me plan for *future* Sundays.

The Pregame Show.   The game hadn't started yet. The TV talk
was mainly about who's playing whom and why. We watched re-
plays of last week's game, which Charlie had already seen before,
but wouldn't think of missing this second time around. I metic-
ulously observed his food requests. He asked for potato chips,

cheese, and crackers. Then peanuts, pretzels, Cokes. I felt like a stadium vendor.

The Game.   Just before the opening kickoff, Charlie asked for the main meal. The teams were ready to play and he was ready to eat. Once the game started, he was all business. No kids. No phone calls. No questions. No jokes. No sex. No interruptions. Nothing but football!

I left extra portions of food on a table near the TV. It didn't seem to matter much what it was. His concentration was singular.

The Halftime.   About an hour later, it was halftime. Charlie turned and looked at me. He vaguely seemed to remember his long-lost wife. Emerging from the room for a few minutes, he blinked the family back into his memory. Then with another sandwich and Coke, he headed back to the gridiron and the second half.

The Two-Minute Warning.   Toward the end of the game I learned another important lesson. The last two minutes of a football game are sacred. Mental note to myself: *Don't serve anything; don't pick up glasses; don't even stir the air!*

In football, as in a whodunit mystery, sometimes you can't tell the good guys from the villains until the last minute, or in this case, the last *two* minutes. Learning this lesson didn't come easy for me, either.

One particular Sunday afternoon, I had made plans to visit friends immediately after the game. With just two minutes to go, I announced, "We'll be waiting in the car for you," and my girls and I headed outside.

Two minutes went by. Then two more minutes. No Charlie. Back inside I went. There he sat, still glued to the tube. "I thought it was over two minutes ago," I began.

"Shhh! Quiet!," he said. "There's only a minute, thirty-seven to go."

"A minute, thirty-seven to go? I've been waiting *five* minutes. How could only a few seconds have elapsed?" I thought, *What kind of logic is that? At this rate, the girls might suffocate in the car by the time the game is over.*

I headed outside to rescue them.

Sudden Death.   "Oh, no!" Charlie screamed from the inside of the house. Fearing the worst, I ran back inside and saw him sitting in the same position, staring at the same game.

"What on earth happened? Are you all right?"

"The Colts just scored in the last ten seconds," he moaned. I breathed a sigh of relief, grateful for the nature of the calamity. I was also glad that the game was finally over.

"Well, c'mon, let's go," I said brightly. "We've been waiting outside for half an hour."

"Go?" he looked at me with unbelieving eyes. "I can't go anywhere. The game is tied. Now it's sudden death!"

"Sudden death?" I wailed. "For whom?"

"That means another fifteen-minute period. First team to score wins the game."

Postgame Show. I later learned that Sudden Death can last an hour. Then the postgame ("What went wrong") show. And the locker-room show. And the wrap-up show. And the scoreboard show. And the interview show. And then finally the highlight show, with each replay from six different angles!

Of course, by the time it's all over, a second game has just begun on another channel.

If you are not a football nut, Sunday afternoons can provide a delicious chunk of time just for you. The only problem then is the constant food supply for the would-be coach in the den, and ofttimes his horde of friends.

I've come up with a solution. Next season I'm going to try intravenous feeding.

The Gang's All Here

Spiced Cider
Shrimp Dip with Crackers
Cocktail Meatballs and Franks
Cheese Ball (shape depends on sport)
Partytime Reubens
Deviled Eggs
Golden Delicious Apple Cake

SPICED CIDER
Serves 8–10

2 quarts apple cider
¼ cup sugar
⅛ teaspoon salt
8 whole cloves

¼ teaspoon ginger
1 teaspoon cinnamon
½ teaspoon nutmeg
Cinnamon sticks

Combine all ingredients except cinnamon sticks in a large saucepan and bring to a boil. Reduce heat to low and simmer for 5 minutes. Strain out spices before serving. Pour into warm mugs and add cinnamon-stick server for each.

SHRIMP DIP

2 pounds cooked, shelled, de-veined shrimp, cut in little pieces
1 cup mayonnaise
¼ cup salad oil
½ onion, chopped fine
3 heaping tablespoons chili sauce
1 teaspoon celery seed

1 garlic clove, minced
1 celery stalk with leaves, chopped
1 teaspoon seasoned salt
2 teaspoons fresh dill, chopped
Dash of Tabasco
Dash of Worcestershire sauce
¼ cup sour cream
1 teaspoon lemon juice

Mix all ingredients and chill 24 hours. Serve on Melba toast or crackers.

COCKTAIL MEATBALLS AND FRANKS
Makes about 100 meatballs

3 pounds ground chuck
1 envelope onion-soup mix
1 4½-ounce can deviled ham (optional)
1 egg, slightly beaten
2 teaspoons monosodium glutamate (optional)
¼ cup dried bread crumbs

1 pound frankfurters, cut in bite-size pieces
2 14-ounce bottles pizza-flavored or hot catsup (regular catsup or chili sauce is fine, too)
1 10-ounce jar apple or grape jelly or apricot preserves

1. In large bowl, mix together ground chuck, onion-soup mix, deviled ham, egg, monosodium glutamate, and bread crumbs. Form into bite-size meatballs. Arrange on cookie sheet; broil under broiler until brown on all sides (or brown in hot fat in skillet). Cool meatballs; cover with plastic wrap; refrigerate. These also freeze well.

2. About 30 minutes before serving: in electric skillet, set at 215°, or in large skillet over medium-low heat, stir together catsup and jelly until blended. Add meatballs and franks; simmer, covered, about 25 minutes or till heated through. Serve in electric skillet, set at warm, or in chafing dish over candle. Or serve in hollowed-out round pumpernickel loaf (looks like a football) with colored toothpicks. Kids of all ages love this!

VARIATION: Bring to a boil contents of 2 10-ounce cans jellied cranberry sauce, 2 12-ounce bottles chili sauce, ¼ cup brown sugar, 2 tablespoons butter, and 2 tablespoons lemon juice. Pour sauce over uncooked meatballs and bake at 350° for 1 hour.

CHEESE BALL
Serves 20

½ pound very sharp Cheddar cheese, shredded
1 8-ounce package cream cheese
2 tablespoons chopped parsley
2 tablespoons chopped onion
1 tablespoon soft butter
⅛ teaspoon salt

1 tablespoon Dijon mustard
2 tablespoons catsup
2 tablespoons apple juice
Dash of Tabasco
1 teaspoon Worcestershire sauce
1 cup chopped pecans or walnuts

Have all ingredients at room temperature. Mix all together except nuts with a wooden spoon. Pack into jars and store in refrigerator; keeps well. Or, mold into football or basketball and roll in chopped pecans. Serve with fancy crackers or Melba toast rounds.

PARTYTIME REUBENS
Makes 3 dozen

1 cup Thousand Island dressing
36 slices party rye bread
1 can well-drained sauerkraut, chopped

1 pound thinly sliced corned beef
½ pound sliced Swiss cheese
Mustard

1. Spread each slice of bread lightly with mustard. Spread ½ teaspoon dressing on each slice of bread. Place 1 tablespoon sauerkraut on each slice of bread, and top with slice of corned beef.

2. Cut cheese the size of bread, and place over corned beef. Arrange sandwiches on baking sheet; bake at 400° for 8 minutes or until cheese melts. Can be made early in day and baked at serving time.

DEVILED EGGS
Makes 12 halves

6 hard-cooked eggs, shelled
¼ cup mayonnaise or salad
    dressing
¼ teaspoon salt
Dash of pepper

1 teaspoon prepared mustard
1 teaspoon minced onion
Paprika
Dash of Tabasco

    1. Cut shelled eggs into lengthwise halves. With teaspoon, carefully remove yolks to small bowl; set whites aside.
    2. Mash yolks until very fine; blend in mayonnaise, salt, pepper, prepared mustard, and onion. Fill hollows of whites, slightly rounding each. Sprinkle with paprika, refrigerate.

GOLDEN DELICIOUS APPLE CAKE
Serves 20
Very, very good.

2 sticks butter
2 cups sugar
2 eggs
8 tablespoons water
2 cups flour
2 teaspoons baking soda
½ teaspoon salt

2 teaspoons cinnamon
½ teaspoon cardamon (optional)
2 teaspoons vanilla
4 cups diced or grated Golden
    Delicious apples
1 cup chopped nuts, divided
⅓ cup brown sugar

    1. Preheat oven to 350°. Beat butter, sugar, eggs, and water together. Stir in flour, soda, salt, and spices.
    2. Add vanilla, apples, and ½ cup nuts. Mix thoroughly. Pour into well-greased and floured 13 x 9 x 2-inch pan. Sprinkle top with ⅓ cup brown sugar and ½ cup nuts. Bake 55 minutes at 350°. Serve with vanilla ice cream.

Halftime Show

Blue Cheese Dip
Coach's Chili
Onion Soup Sticks
Bob Griese's All-Pro Sub
Strawberry Fruit Salad
Ice Cream Balls with
Hot Fudge Sauce

BLUE CHEESE DIP
Makes 1¼ cups

½ cup sour cream
½ cup mayonnaise
3 ounces blue cheese, crumbled

Dash of garlic powder
Dash of paprika
Assorted vegetables cut in strips

Mix all ingredients except vegetables together and chill 2 hours to blend flavors. Serve with vegetables.

COACH'S CHILI
Serves 10–12

3 pounds ground beef
4 tablespoons vegetable or olive oil
2 cups chopped onion
2 tablespoons finely chopped garlic (about 4 cloves)
1 to 2 tablespoons chili powder (or to taste)
1 green pepper, chopped
2 stalks of celery, chopped

2 teaspoons Worcestershire sauce
2 teaspoons cumin (optional)
5 whole cloves
1 tablespoon sugar
½ teaspoon red-pepper flakes or ½ teaspoon Tabasco
1 6-ounce can tomato paste or 2 8-ounce cans tomato sauce

1 teaspoon oregano
3 teaspoons paprika
2 tablespoons chopped green chili peppers (optional)
½ teaspoon freshly ground black pepper
1 bay leaf

1 10½-ounce can beef broth, undiluted
1 28-ounce can tomatoes
2 teaspoons salt
Dash of cinnamon (optional)
2 15-ounce cans kidney beans, drained

1. In a 12-inch skillet, heat 2 tablespoons of the oil. Add meat and cook over high heat for 2 to 3 minutes, stirring, until meat is lightly browned.

2. With a slotted spoon transfer meat to a 4-quart heavy flame-proof casserole or Dutch oven. Add the remaining 2 tablespoons of oil to the skillet and cook onion, garlic, pepper, and celery for 4 to 5 minutes, stirring frequently.

3. Remove skillet from heat, add chili powder, pepper flakes, and stir until onions are well coated with mixture. Then add tomato paste, pour in beef stock, and rest of ingredients except beans. Stir thoroughly and combine with meat in casserole.

4. Bring to boil, stirring once or twice, then half cover pot, turn heat to low and simmer for 1 to 1½ hours.

5. If chili is refrigerated overnight, fat will rise to surface and can be easily skimmed off before reheating. Thirty minutes before serving, add beans and heat.

6. Freeze the leftovers (if any!) for next week's game.

ONION SOUP STICKS
Serves 8

12 slices bread, each cut into 3 strips
¼ cup butter at room temperature

½ package dry onion-soup mix

Mix soup mix and butter together and spread lightly on bread strips. Lay strips on cookie sheet and brown under broiler. Serve hot with chili.

BOB GRIESE'S ALL-PRO SUB
Serves 6
Favorite of the Miami Dolphin quarterback.

4 8-inch submarine rolls
Mayonnaise
Mustard
½ pound cooked Cuban or regular ham, thinly sliced
1 pound roast pork, deli-style, thinly sliced

Sweet pickles, sliced lengthwise
Sweet onions, sliced
¼ pound Swiss cheese, thinly sliced

1. Slice rolls in half and remove some of dough in each section. Spread with mayonnaise on one half, mustard on the other. Put layer of ham, sweet pickle, pork, onion, and cheese on roll. Cover with other half.

2. Toast on buttered grill on both sides until crispy and cheese has melted. Cut each roll in thirds. Makes 12 sections.

STRAWBERRY FRUIT SALAD
Serves 4

2 cups strawberries, sliced in half
1 banana, sliced
4 oranges, peeled and sectioned (save juice)

1 cup pineapple chunks
½ cup brown sugar
½ cup sour cream

Gently toss banana with oranges and reserved juice. Mix strawberries and pineapple; sprinkle with brown sugar. Chill several hours. Combine fruits. Serve in chilled dessert dishes with a spoonful of sour cream.

ICE CREAM BALLS
Makes 24 balls

3 quarts of ice cream (coffee, peppermint, or your favorite flavors)

The day before, make round, firm balls with ice cream scoop and place on cookie sheet in freezer. (Dip scoop in glass of warm water after making each one.) Allow balls to freeze firmly. Store them in plastic bags, or, if making them the day before party, place sheet of foil gently over them. Serve in pretty, chilled bowl, alternating colors of ice cream.

Hot Fudge Sauce

2 tablespoons butter	½ cup evaporated milk
2 squares chocolate	½ teaspoon vanilla
¾ cup sugar	

Melt butter and chocolate. Add sugar and milk. Cook over hot water 15 minutes. Add vanilla. Serve warm over ice cream balls.

VARIATIONS: Ice cream balls may be rolled in toasted, chopped pecans or almonds and kept in freezer. At Christmastime, vanilla balls may be rolled in broken peppermint candy.

Uh-Oh-Overtime

Easy Seafood Bisque
Tie-Breaker Burgers with Mustard Butter
French Onion Casserole
Potato Chips
Assorted Pickles
Chocolate Frosted Brownies

If the whole gang decides to stay on for the postpost game show, you'll be ready for them.

EASY SEAFOOD BISQUE
Serves 6

2 tablespoons butter
1 onion, chopped finely
1 clove garlic, minced
1 10¾-ounce can cream of mushroom soup, undiluted
1 10¾-ounce can tomato soup, undiluted
1 7-ounce can crab meat

2 cups milk (you may use 1 cup of milk and 1 cup of cream)
1 tablespoon Worcestershire sauce
¼ teaspoon cayenne
2 teaspoons curry powder (optional)

Sauté onion and garlic in butter. Add rest of ingredients. Heat over low heat. Serve, sprinkled with chopped parsley.

TIE-BREAKER BURGERS
Serves 6

1½ tablespoons butter	1 teaspoon salt
1 shallot or small onion peeled and finely chopped	⅛ teaspoon pepper
	1 tablespoon butter or margarine
2 pounds ground beef chuck	6 hamburger buns, buttered and
1½ tablespoons Worcestershire sauce	toasted

1. Sauté shallot in butter until tender. Place meat in a large bowl. Add shallot mixture, Worcestershire sauce, salt and pepper. Shape meat into six 1-inch thick patties.

2. Heat 1 tablespoon butter in a skillet over moderately high heat. Cook patties for about 4 to 8 minutes, depending on desired degree of doneness. Turn once during cooking. Serve on buns with pat of mustard butter on each.

MUSTARD BUTTER

⅓ cup butter (sweet preferred) at room temperature	½ teaspoon chopped fresh tarragon or ⅛ teaspoon dried tarragon leaves
2 tablespoons chopped fresh parsley	1 tablespoon Dijon mustard

In small bowl, add parsley and tarragon to butter and mix well. Blend in mustard. Place butter mixture on wax paper and spread evenly. Chill until firm. Cut butter into 6 pieces and place one piece of each on cooked hamburgers.

FRENCH ONION CASSEROLE
Serves 6

4 medium onions, sliced
3 tablespoons butter
2 tablespoons flour
Dash of pepper
1 cup beef bouillon
1½ cups plain croutons

2 tablespoons butter, melted
2 ounces process Swiss cheese,
   shredded (½ cup)
3 tablespoons grated Parmesan
   cheese

1. Cook onions in 3 tablespoons butter just until tender. Blend in flour and pepper. Add bouillon, cook and stir till thickened and bubbly.
2. Turn into 1-quart casserole. Toss croutons with 2 tablespoons melted butter; spoon on top onion mixture. Sprinkle with Swiss and Parmesan cheese.
3. Place under broiler just till cheese melts, about 1 minute. Serve immediately. Yummy!

CHOCOLATE FROSTED BROWNIES
Makes 24

3 or 4 squares unsweetened
   chocolate
½ cup butter (one stick)
½ cup vegetable shortening
2 teaspoons instant coffee
   powder
4 eggs

½ teaspoon salt
2 cups sugar
1 tablespoon vanilla
1 cup sifted flour
½ cup chocolate chips
1 cup chopped nuts (optional)

1. Preheat oven to 350°. Butter 13 x 9-inch baking pan. Melt butter, shortening and chocolate together over low heat. Mix together and let cool. Stir in coffee powder.
2. Beat eggs with salt. Add sugar slowly and beat until very light. Stir in chocolate mixture and vanilla.
3. Add flour all at once and mix just until smooth by hand. Stir

in chocolate chips and nuts. Bake 40 minutes. Cut into squares while hot.

Brownies are scrumptious as is, but you may want to completely captivate your gang by serving them frosted.

CHOCOLATE FROSTING

2 tablespoons butter
1 square unsweetened chocolate
2 tablespoons warm water or milk

1 tablespoon vanilla
2 cups sifted powdered sugar
Pecan or walnut halves

Melt butter and chocolate together over low heat. Stir in water and vanilla. Remove from heat and stir in sugar until smooth. Frost cooled brownies and top each with nut halves.

Victory Party

MUSHROOMS AND SHRIMP WITH
SAUCE REMOULADE
Serves 25

2 pounds large white mushrooms, washed and dried
1½ pounds medium shrimp,
   cooked, peeled, and
   deveined
3 tablespoons minced parsley
3 tablespoons minced shallots
3 tablespoons minced celery
2 tablespoons minced green
   pepper
2 cloves garlic, minced

6 tablespoons Dijon or hot
   mustard
2 tablespoons chopped capers,
   well drained
2 tablespoons prepared
   horseradish
1 tablespoon vinegar
1 tablespoon salad oil
¼ teaspoon Tabasco
2 cups mayonnaise

Combine all ingredients except mayonnaise, mushrooms, and shrimp in electric blender; process about 1 minute. Stir mayonnaise into blended mixture. Chill. Serve sauce as a dip surrounded with mushrooms in basket and shrimp on platter.

CHAMPIONSHIP LASAGNE
Serves 10

MEAT SAUCE INGREDIENTS

¼ cup salad or olive oil
1 cup onion, chopped
2 garlic cloves, minced
1 pound ground beef
¾ pound sweet or hot Italian sausage (4 links removed from their casings)
¼ cup chopped parsley
1 28-ounce can tomatoes
1 12-ounce can tomato paste

1 6-ounce can tomato sauce
½ cup water or beef broth
1 tablespoon sugar
1 teaspoon oregano
1½ teaspoons dried basil leaves
1 teaspoon salt
½ teaspoon pepper
⅛ teaspoon fennel seeds (optional)

REMAINING INGREDIENTS

¾ of l-pound package lasagne noodles (about 12 noodles)
½ pound mozzarella cheese, shredded

1 pound ricotta cheese
1 cup cream-style cottage cheese
1 egg, beaten
1 cup grated Parmesan cheese

1. Heat oil in large saucepan or skillet. Add onion to garlic and sauté until tender but not brown. Add ground beef and sausage and stir until crumbly and brown. Pour off fat. Add rest of sauce ingredients and bring to boil; reduce heat and cook slowly uncovered for 2 hours; stir occasionally. Make meat sauce the day before, if possible. Long, slow cooking enhances the flavor.

2. In large bowl, mix together ricotta, cottage cheese, and egg.

3. In 8-quart kettle, bring 3 quarts water to boiling. Stir in 1 tablespoon salt and 1 tablespoon oil. Add lasagne, 2 or 3 at a time, so water does not stop boiling. Boil uncovered, stirring occasionally, 10 minutes. Drain in colander; rinse with cold water. Dry on dish towels.

4. Preheat oven to 375°. In bottom of 13 x 9-inch baking dish, spoon 1 cup meat sauce. Place 6 lasagne noodles, overlapping each, over sauce. Spread with half of ricotta mixture; sprinkle with ⅔ cup mozzarella cheese. Spoon 1½ cups sauce over cheese; sprinkle with

¼ cup Parmesan. Repeat layering with rest of noodles, ricotta, mozzarella, and Parmesan cheeses.

5. If freezing, wrap dish tightly with foil. Thaw before baking. Cover loosely with foil. Bake 45 minutes. Remove foil and bake 15 minutes longer until bubbly and lightly browned on top. Cool 15 minutes before cutting into squares.

BIBB LETTUCE SALAD
Serves 8

6 heads Bibb lettuce washed, dried, and broken into pieces
3 tomatoes cut in wedges or 16 cherry tomatoes
1 egg yolk
⅓ cup lemon juice
½ teaspoon salt
½ teaspoon pepper
⅔ cup olive oil
1 clove garlic, minced (optional)
⅓ cup chopped scallions
⅔ cup grated Parmesan cheese
½ cup cooked crumbled bacon
1 cup croutons

1. Beat egg yolk, lemon juice, salt, and pepper with wire whisk. Add olive oil slowly, beating constantly until sauce is creamy. Stir in garlic, scallions, and ⅓ cup cheese.

2. To serve, toss lettuce, tomatoes and croutons with dressing and pile evenly on 8 chilled salad plates. Sprinkle bacon and remaining cheese over top.

CHOCOLATE ROYALE FONDUE
Serves 8

1 6-ounce package semisweet chocolate morsels
2 squares unsweetened chocolate
½ cup sugar
1⅓ cups light or heavy cream
2 tablespoons butter
Dash of salt
6 marshmallows
Dash of cinnamon (optional)
1-inch squares of pound cake
Pineapple and banana chunks
Apple and orange slices
Seedless green grapes
Strawberries
Dried apricots

Melt all chocolate in top of double boiler. Add next six ingredients and stir until smooth and thickened. Pour into fondue pot or chafing dish. Spear cubes of cake or fruit with fondue forks and dip into fondue.

8
For Women Only

Light and Breezy
Super Shower
Committee Confab
Christmas Coffee

The Soup Operas

Luncheon with the girls sure beats watching the soaps. It's so nice when everything is live and in living color, with no commercials. At lunch, the action starts quickly and then heats up from there. Word from "The Diet Corner" usually begins when the 75,000-calorie chocolate soufflé is being taken from the oven. While the soufflé is being devoured, discussion continues concerning six new foolproof diets, none of which requires any cutback whatever in consumption. Last Wednesday's "All Chocolate Diet," for example, was credited to a Kansas City mother who reportedly lost an aggregate of 3,465 pounds over nineteen years, before she died in a size 22 dress with a smile on her face.

And there's the "Ripoff of the Week Award," which is given after thorough discussion of the roofer's bill, the vet's bill, and the Reliable Mail Order House. The award last week went to the mechanic who charged $87 for the same brake-job he had fixed for $132 only three weeks before. He explained the grease-stained tab to Betty Ann by saying, "Look, lady, it's okay. Just trust me!"

But the real live action starts right after lunch, and continues until the next-to-the-last person leaves. The girls' stories are exciting, bloodcurdling, and romantic. On the other hand, they are dull, repetitious, and boring, depending upon whether you are first or last to hear.

The stories are also true (or at least that's what they all say). Being married to a lawyer, I know there are three sides to every story—her side, his side, and the truth. Her side is usually the most juicy. In fact, I've thought about writing soap operas, being careful, of course, to change the names to confuse the neighbors.

For the morning shows, I've thought about starting with "The Great Cornflake Cleanup," followed by "General Housework," and "The Housewives." Very little dialogue necessary for these shows, since the TV is competing with the whining vacuum cleaner and sloshing clothes washer.

The noontime-can't-miss favorite is "The Young and the Rundown," featuring a twenty-seven-year-old Dallas housewife who is ready for her 200,000-mile checkup.

The afternoon shows will feature "Guiding Car Pools" and "All

My Active Children." Then follows "As the Pizza Burns," "Search for Tostados," and closing with the late-afternoon, sure-fire winner, "Edge of Aspirin."

For the insomniacs, I believe a late-night show like "Dazed All Our Lives" would give the "Tonight Show" fits, and "Love of Sleep" might even make Tom Snyder nervous.

At first, I was concerned about having enough fresh material for all these shows, but I'm sure that won't be a problem. If I run dry, I'll just take good notes at lunch.

At these sessions I've discovered that usually more questions are raised than resolved. Like yesterday at Brenda's. Where did we leave off? Oh, yes, will Sue find true happiness in her Cuisinart? Will Bill marry the cute blonde secretary, Janet? Or will Bill remarry Bonnie? And will Bonnie remarry Bill if Bill will remarry Bonnie?

Why did Bonnie develop lower-back pains when handsome Dr. Edwards opened up his office on Elm? Why does Dr. Seuss, Bonnie's uncle, feel threatened by lower-back-pain doctors?

Why are Bonnie's back pains becoming worse as her treatments increase? Why does Dr. Edwards's secretary, Janet, leave early in Bill's car, while Bonnie's car is still in the doctor's parking lot? Can Dr. Edwards treat back pains in the dark?

For these questions and more, don't miss lunch next Tuesday at Gail's (she lives next door to Dr. Edwards). Please bring your favorite dish, as Gail can't cook, since her neck pains started Saturday night. . . .

Light and Breezy

GAZPACHO
Serves 6
Takes 15 minutes to prepare

2 large tomatoes (1¾ pounds) peeled, or 1 can whole tomatoes
1 large cucumber, pared and halved
1 medium onion, peeled and halved
1 medium green pepper, quartered and seeded
1 pimento, drained
2 cups V-8 or tomato juice
½ 10½-ounce can beef bouillon, undiluted
2 teaspoons Worcestershire sauce

¼ cup salad oil
Pinch of sugar
⅓ cup red-wine vinegar
¼ teaspoon dry mustard
Few drops Tabasco
1½ teaspoons salt
Red food coloring, if desired
Dash of coarsely ground black pepper

OPTIONAL:
2 cloves garlic, split
2 tablespoons salad oil
¾ cup packaged croutons
¼ cup chopped chives

1. In electric blender, combine tomatoes, half the cucumber, half the onion, the pimento, and ½ cup tomato juice. Blend, covered and at high speed, 30 seconds, to puree vegetables.

2. Chop remaining vegetables finely with sharp knife. (If you

have a food processor, put *all* the vegetables in it, and let it do the chopping.)

3. In large bowl, mix pureed and chopped vegetables with remaining tomato juice, beef bouillon, oil, vinegar, Worcestershire sauce, sugar, Tabasco, dry mustard, salt, and black pepper. Stir in few drops of red food coloring. Refrigerate mixture, covered, until it is well chilled, at least 6 hours. Also, refrigerate 6 serving bowls.

4. Meanwhile, rub inside of small skillet with split garlic cloves. Add 2 tablespoons oil; heat. Sauté the croutons in oil until browned. Set aside.

5. Serve Gazpacho in chilled bowls. Sprinkle with chopped chives and croutons.

TIP: To save time and trouble, you can blend all of the vegetables in the blender, except the green pepper, which when blended, turns the soup an ugly color. Chop the pepper very fine, and add to Gazpacho.

QUICHE À LA MORGAN
Serves 6–8

2 onions, peeled and thinly sliced
1 tablespoon butter
4 eggs
1⅓ cups half-and-half or light cream
¼ teaspoon nutmeg
¼ teaspoon pepper (white preferred)
⅛ teaspoon hot pepper sauce
⅛ teaspoon dry mustard
½ pound bacon slices, cooked and crumbled
1 9-inch unbaked pie shell
1½ cups shredded Gruyère cheese or Swiss cheese

1. Preheat oven to 400°. Sauté onions in butter. Set aside.

2. In large bowl, beat eggs slightly. Beat in cream, nutmeg, pepper, hot pepper sauce, and dry mustard until well blended. Set aside.

3. Sprinkle bacon over bottom of unbaked pie shell. Sprinkle onions over bacon. Then sprinkle cheeses evenly over onions. If not baking immediately, refrigerate. (This can be done early in the day.)

4. One hour before serving, pour in egg mixture. Place in oven,

reduce heat to 350°. Bake for 40 minutes or until puffed and golden. Let pie cool on wire rack 15 to 30 minutes, then cut into wedges and serve. Delicious hot or cold.

VARIATION: Mix 1 cup chopped fresh spinach into cream mixture. Omit sautéed onions.

SPINACH SALAD BOWL
Serves 6

1 10-ounce bag fresh spinach	½ teaspoon salt
1 head Boston lettuce	3 hard-cooked eggs, chopped
8 slices bacon	1 cup freshly grated Parmesan
⅓ cup chopped shallots or green onions	cheese
	1 tablespoon seasoned salad salt
½ cup red-wine vinegar	(optional)
2 tablespoons brown sugar	Freshly ground pepper
½ teaspoon Worcestershire sauce	Red onion rings (optional)
	6 daisies (optional)

1. Trim and clean spinach and lettuce under cold running water. Shake dry in salad basket or tea towel. Tear in bite-size pieces and put in serving dish (or wash and dry early in day and keep in plastic bag in refrigerator).

2. Fry bacon in large skillet until crisp. Drain on paper towels. Reserve ¼ cup bacon fat. When cool, crumble bacon. Set aside.

3. Sauté shallots in ¼ cup bacon fat until lightly browned. Add the vinegar, sugar, salt, and Worcestershire sauce. Bring to a boil. Pour over greens and toss lightly to coat. Sprinkle with eggs, bacon, and Parmesan cheese.

4. Garnish with red-onion rings. Arrange daisies around edge of large salad bowl or one on top of each individual salad.

TIP: On another occasion you may wish to serve this yummy salad as a main course. Just add hot bread, dessert, and beverage.

STRAWBERRIES À LA MODE
Serves 6

1 quart ripe strawberries,   ¼ cup raspberry sherbert, slightly
   washed and dried on towels   softened
1 tablespoon sugar   1 cup heavy whipping cream
1 cup vanilla ice cream, slightly   1 teaspoon powdered sugar
   softened

1. Set six large berries aside. Slice remaining berries and put in a glass bowl. Sprinkle sugar over top. Cover and refrigerate about 3 hours.

2. Whip cream and sweeten with 1 teaspoon powered sugar. To serve, mix ice cream and sherbert into berries. Spoon into chilled sherbert glasses. Spoon whipped cream on top. Garnish with whole berries. Serve immediately.

LEMON ANGEL PIE
Serves 6–8

1½ cups granulated sugar   3 tablespoons lemon or lime
¼ teaspoon cream of tartar   juice
4 egg whites, at room   2 tablespoons grated lemon or
   temperature   lime rind
1 teaspoon vanilla   ⅛ teaspoon salt
2 tablespoons toasted coconut   1 cup heavy cream
   (optional)   6 strawberries for decoration
4 egg yolks   (optional)

1. Preheat oven to 275°. Sift 1 cup sugar with ¼ teaspoon cream of tartar. Beat egg whites until they stand in stiff, not dry, peaks. Slowly add sugar, beating continually.

2. When meringue makes very stiff, glossy peaks, spread it over bottom and sides, of well-buttered 9- or 10-inch pie plate, making sides 1 inch thick. Sprinkle rim with 2 tablespoons coconut. Bake 1 hour until light brown. Cool.

3. Beat 4 egg yolks until thick and lemon colored. Stir in ½ cup sugar, lemon juice, grated lemon rind, and salt. Cook in top of double boiler over boiling water, stirring constantly until thick, about 8 to 10 minutes. Cool. Whip cream, and fold into mixture.

4. Slowly pour cool lemon-cream mixture into center of meringue, making sure that all little pockets are filled. Smooth top. Chill at least 12 hours, preferably 24, before garnishing it for serving. If desired, top with globs of additional sweetened whipped cream and strawberries.

TIP: To bring egg whites to room temperature quickly, set bowl of whites in warm water.

SPICED ICED TEA
Serves 6–8

4 Constant Comment Tea bags   **6 Sweet 'N Low packets**
4 regular tea bags   **6 tablespoons sugar**
10 cups boiling water

Steep tea bags in boiling water 5 minutes. Remove bags. Add sweetener and sugar. Stir to dissolve. Cool. Add small amount of cold water to dilute to desired strength. Pour over ice-filled tumblers. Garnish with lemon or orange slice and a mint sprig.

Super Shower

PARTY CHICKEN SALAD IN PINEAPPLE SHELLS OR MELONS
Serves 8

4 small ripe pineapples or melons
Juice of 1 lemon
4 cups diced cooked or canned chicken
1½ cups sliced celery
1½ cups halved green grapes, seeds removed
1 cup mayonnaise or salad dressing

1 cup heavy cream, whipped
½ teaspoon salt
¼ teaspoon marjoram (optional)
1 cup slivered almonds or whole blanched almonds toasted in 350° oven for 5 minutes
Grated orange rind (optional)

1. Cut pineapples (including crowns) in half. Hollow out, leaving shell ½ inch thick. Remove and discard core from pineapple; dice remaining fruit.

2. Lightly mix together chicken, 1 cup pineapple, celery, grapes, and half of almonds. Fold whipped cream into mayonnaise and add salt and marjoram. Gently fold into chicken mixture. Chill at least one hour.

3. At serving time, fill pineapple halves or melon halves with chicken salad. Sprinkle remaining almonds and grated orange rind

on top. Place each half on lettuce-lined salad plate, with green grape cluster, if desired. For a charming touch, tuck in a pretty flower on each pineapple or melon.

ORANGE MUFFINS
Makes 16

1 tablespoon flour	½ cup sugar
¼ cup brown sugar	1 teaspoon grated orange peel
½ teaspoon cinnamon	⅔ cup orange juice
1 tablespoon butter, melted	½ cup butter, melted
2 cups flour	2 eggs, beaten slightly
2 teaspoons baking powder	1 teaspoon vanilla
1 teaspoon salt	½ cup coarsely chopped walnuts
¼ teaspoon baking soda	

1. Mix first four ingredients in small bowl and set aside for topping.
2. Line 16 muffin cups with cupcake papers or grease 16 3-inch muffin-pan cups.
3. In large bowl, mix together flour, baking powder, baking soda, salt, sugar, and orange peel. Stir in all at one time, the orange juice, melted butter, eggs, vanilla, and walnuts, just until blended.
4. Spoon batter into muffin-pan cups. Sprinkle on topping. Bake 20 to 25 minutes or until cake tester, inserted in center of one of muffins, comes out clean. Loosen with spatula and lift muffins onto rack.

HEAVENLY REFRIGERATOR ROLLS
Makes 30

2 packages active dry yeast	½ cup shortening
1¼ cups warm water	½ cup sugar
3 eggs, well beaten	2 teaspoons salt
4½ to 5 cups flour	Butter

1. Stir and dissolve yeast in ¼ cup warm water. Let stand 10 minutes. Combine dissolved yeast, eggs, 2½ cups flour, 1 cup warm water, shortening, sugar, and salt in a large mixer bowl. Beat until smooth at medium speed, scraping sides of bowl, for 2 minutes.

2. With wooden spoon, stir in remaining flour to make soft dough. Cover. Let rise until double in bulk, about 1 hour. Punch down, refrigerate overnight.

3. Three hours before baking, divide dough in half. Roll each half into a ½ inch thick rectangle. Spread with butter. Starting with long side, roll up jelly-roll style. Cut in 1-inch slices. Place in greased muffin-pan cups, cut side down.

4. Cover. Let rise 3 hours until doubled. Bake in 400° oven 12 to 15 minutes.

VARIATION:

CINNAMON PECAN ROLLS

4 tablespoons butter	**1 tablespoon butter, melted**
½ cup brown sugar	**2 teaspoons granulated sugar**
1 tablespoon light corn syrup	**½ teaspoon cinnamon**
½ cup chopped pecans	

1. Follow Heavenly Refrigerator Roll recipe through step 3, but do not place dough in muffin-pan cups. In small saucepan, melt 4 tablespoons butter; remove from heat and stir in brown sugar and corn syrup.

2. Divide brown sugar mixture among 30 well-greased muffin pans; sprinkle with pecans. Place slice of dough in each. Brush rolls with 1 tablespoon butter. Combine granulated sugar and cinnamon; sprinkle over rolls.

3. Cover. Let rise till double, about 3 hours. Bake in 400° oven for 12 to 15 minutes. Invert onto racks.

OLD-FASHIONED STRAWBERRY BUTTER

2 sticks sweet butter	**1 cup strawberries, washed, with**
6 tablespoons powdered sugar	**hulls removed**

Mix ingredients in blender. Use on hot biscuits, English muffins, or waffles.

OLD-FASHIONED PEACH BUTTER

3 pounds fully ripe peaches 1½ teaspoons lemon juice
¾ cup water ⅛ teaspoon ground cinnamon
2¼ cups sugar Dash of ground cloves

1. Wash peaches and remove skins. (Dipping the fruit in boiling water, then quickly in cold water makes peeling easier.) Halve peaches, remove pits; dice (makes about 1½ quarts). In 5-quart saucepot, heat water; add peaches and cook, covered, until mushy, about 20 minutes.

2. In blender puree half the peaches; pour puree into saucepot. Reheat with remaining half. Measure fruit pulp and for each two cups, add 1½ cups sugar. (Makes 3 cups pulp.)

3. Add lemon juice, cinnamon, and cloves to fruit pulp. Heat, stirring, over low heat until sugar dissolves. Then cook slowly until quite thick, about 1 hour, stirring occasionally. As mixture thickens, stir frequently to prevent sticking.

FRUIT SALAD IN MERINGUE NEST
Serves 10

6 egg whites (at room
  temperature)
1½ cups sugar
½ teaspoon white vinegar
1 cup strawberry halves
½ cup blueberries
½ cantaloupe, shaped into
  balls
1 cup pineapple chunks, bananas, or any other fruit

1 pint vanilla ice cream
1 cup heavy cream, whipped
2 tablespoons sugar
1 teaspoon vanilla
2 tablespoons chopped crystallized ginger
½ cup chopped macadamia nuts
  or pecans

1. Preheat oven to 275°. Beat egg whites until soft peaks form. Add sugar, 2 tablespoons at a time, beating constantly until glossy and stiff. Beat in vinegar.

2. Spread in well-buttered, 9-inch spring-form pan or 9-inch cake pan and bake 1 hour. Cool on rack (center drops as it cools). Gently loosen pan and remove sides. (You can also store meringue in a cookie tin for 2 or 3 days.)

3. Beat cream, add sugar and vanilla, beating until stiff. Refrigerate. Mix fruit and ginger. Chill.

4. Just before serving, place meringue on cake stand or serving dish. Cover top of meringue with thin slices of vanilla ice cream. Spoon fruit onto ice cream and spoon whipped cream on top. Sprinkle with nuts.

SHERBERT-ICE-CREAM CAKE
Serves 10–12

1½ pints raspberry sherbert
1½ pints orange sherbert
1½ pints pistachio ice cream or lime sherbert
3 quarts vanilla ice cream
2 cups chopped pecans
2 cups shaved semisweet-chocolate squares, or coarsely chopped semisweet-chocolate pieces

1 pint whipping cream
Green or red food coloring (optional)
1 pint fresh strawberries (optional)

1. With ice-cream scoop, make 8 rounded balls from each of raspberry, orange and pistachio flavors (total of 24 balls). Place balls on chilled cookie sheet with slight stand-up edge; freeze very firm.

2. Chill in freezer a 10-inch angel-food-cake pan, 4 inches deep.

3. In large bowl, with wooden spoon or electric mixer, beat 1½ quarts vanilla ice cream until softened and like a heavy batter; stir in 1 cup chopped pecans and 1 cup shaved or chopped chocolate. Spoon enough of vanilla ice-cream mixture into chilled angel-cake pan to make 1 inch layer. Quickly arrange half of raspberry, orange,

and pistachio balls on top, alternating them against center tube and side of cake pan. Spoon rest of vanilla ice-cream mixture over balls. Return to freezer.

4. Beat up remaining 1½ quarts vanilla ice cream as in step 3; add rest of pecans and chocolate.

5. Continue alternating rest of raspberry, orange and pistachio balls, then cover with vanilla ice-cream mixture; cake pan will be full. Cover with foil. Return to freezer.

6. On serving day, cover a 10-inch circle of cardboard with foil.

7. Remove angel-cake pan from freezer; run knife around edges of pan and inner tube.

8. Quickly dip cake pan in and out of lukewarm water. Lay foil-covered cardboard circle (or serving plate that fits in freezer) over top of pan; invert pan; then unmold ice cream. Return to freezer.

9. Whip cream, adding a few drops of green or red food color to tint delicate green or pink.

10. Remove ice-cream cake from freezer. Quickly frost with tinted whipped cream, then return to freezer until serving time.

11. To serve, place cake on serving plate, if not done earlier. Garnish with strawberries.

Committee Confab

Hot Chicken Salad
Caramelized Baked Peaches
Avocado and Citrus Salad
Refrigerator Bran Muffins
Chocolate Mousse Pie

HOT CHICKEN SALAD
Serves 8

4 cups diced, freshly cooked chicken or turkey
2 cups thinly sliced celery
½ cup finely chopped green peppers (optional)
½ cup grated Cheddar cheese
4 tablespoons lemon juice
1 teaspoon Accent (optional)
1 teaspoon salt

⅔ cup coarsely chopped walnuts or almonds
½ cup mayonnaise or enough to moisten
½ cup cream of chicken soup, undiluted
1 tablespoon onion, finely minced

Mix lightly together and pile into 2-quart shallow baking dish or 13 x 9-inch dish.

TOPPING

1 cup prepared stuffing mix or crushed potato chips

½ cup grated Cheddar cheese
4 tablespoons butter, melted

Mix together topping ingredients and sprinkle on top. Bake at 400° for 20 minutes. (If you prepare salad early in the day, sprinkle on topping just before baking).

CARAMELIZED BAKED PEACHES

1 large can cling peach halves,   ¼ cup powdered sugar
    drained   2 teaspoons butter, melted

Sift powdered sugar over peach halves. Place in buttered baking dish. Drizzle butter over peaches. Bake at 400° for 20 minutes or until sugar turns brown and crisp.

AVOCADO AND CITRUS SALAD
Serves 6–8

2 grapefruit, peeled and   ½ teaspoon sugar
    sectioned   ¾ teaspoon chili sauce
2 oranges, peeled and sectioned   ¾ teaspoon catsup
1 head Boston lettuce   ¼ teaspoon prepared mustard
1 avocado   1½ teaspoons lemon juice
1 red onion (optional)   ½ teaspoon Worcestershire
½ cup salad or olive oil   sauce
2 tablespoons cider vinegar   ¼ teaspoon prepared
1 teaspoon salt   horseradish
Dash of pepper   Dash of Tabasco
⅛ teaspoon paprika   ½ clove garlic, peeled
Dash of celery salt

1. Line a salad bowl with washed, crisped Boston lettuce leaves. Arrange orange and grapefruit sections in two rows. (Or use individual salad plates.)

2. Peel and slice avocado lengthwise and dip in grapefruit or lemon juice. Arrange in a row next to grapefruit. Cut 3 or 4 slices from a red onion. Separate into rings and arrange next to avocado slices. Refrigerate, covered with plastic wrap.

3. Make dressing: In jar with tight-fitting lid combine rest of ingredients. Shake until completely blended. Refrigerate several hours. At serving time, remove garlic, shake well, and spoon over salad.

REFRIGERATOR BRAN MUFFINS

1 cup Bran Buds cereal
1 cup boiling water
2 cups All-Bran cereal, divided
½ cup sugar
½ cup oil
2 eggs
1 cup molasses

2½ cups all-purpose flour (half
   whole wheat, if desired)
2½ teaspoons soda
1 teaspoon salt
2 cups buttermilk
1 cup chopped dates or raisins

1. Pour boiling water over 1 cup Bran Buds; stir to moisten and set aside to cool.

2. Cream sugar and oil until light and fluffy; add eggs, one at a time, beating well, and molasses.

3. Combine flour, soda, and salt; add to creamed mixture alternately with buttermilk; stir in dates or raisins.

4. Blend in cereal and water mixture and remaining 2 cups cereal. Store in tightly covered jar in refrigerator until ready to use, up to five or six weeks.

5. When ready to bake, spoon batter into greased muffin tins or cupcake liners ⅔ full and bake at 400° for 20 minutes. Muffins freeze well, too.

CHOCOLATE MOUSSE PIE
Serves 8–10

4 tablespoons finely chopped
   pecans, divided
8 eggs, separated
⅛ teaspoon salt
1 or 2 tablespoons powdered
   coffee

1 cup sugar
3 squares unsweetened chocolate, melted and cooled
½ cup heavy cream

1. Grease 9-inch pie plate well and sprinkle with 3 tablespoons pecans; set aside. In large mixing bowl, beat egg whites at high speed until stiff but not dry; set aside.

2. In small mixing bowl, mix egg yolks, salt, and coffee. Add

sugar gradually and beat at high speed until thick and light-colored. Add chocolate and beat until well blended.

3. Stir a fourth of whites into chocolate mixture, then pour chocolate mixture over remaining whites and fold in gently but thoroughly. Pour about half of mixture into prepared pie plate to ½ inch from rim; bake in preheated 350° oven 18 to 20 minutes, or until still slightly moist when pick is inserted in center; cool on rack.

4. Whip cream just until soft peaks form; fold into remaining mousse and chill. Spoon whipped-cream mixture onto cooled, baked mousse and chill overnight. Just before serving, decorate with dollops of whipped cream and sprinkle with remaining pecans.

Christmas Coffee

> Quick Eggnog Royale
> Salted Pecans
> Holiday Coffee Cake
> with Cinnamon Nut Topping
> Cheese Tray with Strawberries
> Christmas Snowballs
> Russian Tea
> Golden Pineapple Centerpiece

QUICK EGGNOG ROYALE
Makes 30 ½-cup servings

2 pints coffee ice cream
2 quarts eggnog
3 cups cold coffee

1 pint whipping cream
Dash of nutmeg

1. Day before, scoop out 10 large ice-cream balls; refreeze on cookie sheet. Chill eggnog.
2. Just before serving, stir eggnog and coffee into large chilled, punchbowl. Whip cream in medium bowl just until soft peaks form; fold into eggnog mixture. Place ice-cream balls on top and sprinkle with nutmeg.

SALTED PECANS
Makes about 4 cups

1½ pounds shelled pecans
1 tablespoon salt

6 tablespoons unsalted butter, melted and cooled

1. Preheat oven to 350°. Place nuts in large mixing bowl and pour butter over them. Toss with wooden spoon until all nuts glisten, then toss with salt. Transfer nuts to shallow roasting pan and spread in one layer.

2. Roast nuts uncovered 15 to 20 minutes, tossing them from time to time with wooden spoon. When nuts are crisp and golden brown, transfer to paper towels to drain. Cool to room temperature and serve at once, or store in airtight jar in cool place.

HOLIDAY COFFEE CAKE
Serves 10–14

1 cup soft butter	1½ teaspoons baking soda
2 cups sugar	1½ teaspoons baking powder
3 eggs	1¼ teaspoons salt
2 teaspoons vanilla	1½ cups sour cream
3 cups flour	

1. Preheat oven to 350°. Grease 10-inch tube or Bundt pan. Combine butter, sugar, eggs, and vanilla; beat at medium speed for 2 minutes.

2. Mix all dry ingredients. Alternately add with sour cream into first mixture.

3. Put ½ of batter into pan, then sprinkle on ½ of topping. Pour remainder of batter into pan and sprinkle with remaining topping. Bake for 1 hour or until cake pulls away from pan.

CINNAMON NUT TOPPING

¾ cup dried bread crumbs	1½ teaspoons cinnamon
½ cup flour	½ teaspoon nutmeg
½ cup butter	1 cup pecans or walnuts,
⅔ cup brown sugar	chopped

Mix all together until crumbly.

CHEESE TRAY WITH STRAWBERRIES
Serves 12

3 8-ounce packages cream cheese	1 quart unhulled, whole strawberries
6 tablespoons light brown sugar	Crisp assorted crackers
1½ teaspoon cinnamon	

1. Wash strawberries gently, and place on paper towels to dry.
2. Form cream cheese into a thick roll. Mix sugar and cinnamon and sprinkle over roll. Place roll on serving tray; surround with strawberries, piled high. Put crackers at one end of tray or in pretty bowl. To serve, dip berry into cream cheese and eat with a cracker.

CHRISTMAS SNOWBALLS
Makes 50 cookies

1 cup butter, at room temperature	2¼ cups sifted flour
½ cup powdered sugar	¼ teaspoon salt
2 teaspoons vanilla	1 cup finely chopped nuts

1. Combine butter, sugar, and vanilla, and beat until fluffy. Sift together flour and salt, and stir into butter mixture. Stir in nuts.
2. Chill dough several hours. Preheat oven to 400°. Roll into balls about the size of large marble. Place balls 2½ inches apart on an ungreased cookie sheet. Bake in middle of oven until set, but not browned (about 10 to 12 minutes).
3. While still warm, roll balls gently in powdered sugar. Place on cookie rack and cool. Sift powdered sugar over cookies again.

RUSSIAN TEA
Serves 25

3 quarts boiling water	2 teaspoons whole cloves
1½ cups sugar	4 cinnamon sticks
Juice and grated rind of one lemon	1½ tablespoons loose tea
	¼ teaspoon allspice
Juice and grated rind of 2 oranges	1 6-ounce can frozen lemonade, undiluted

Heat first 6 ingredients, and keep hot (not boiling) for 20 minutes. Add tea. Let stand 5 minutes. Stir in all spices and lemonade. Strain. Store in refrigerator and reheat when guests drop by during the holiday season.

GOLDEN PINEAPPLE CENTERPIECE

For a pretty, inexpensive centerpiece for your table, spray a fresh pineapple with gold paint, letting top remain green. Place pineapple on green leaves arranged on tray, and surround with bananas, lemons, and nuts (or any fruit you choose). The pineapple will keep a week.

9
Balancing the Calories

Painless Pizza
Figure Formula
Spa Special
Slim, but Fun

Diary of a Short-Order Cook and Cabbie

Take last Saturday, for example. (Please do; I'd rather forget it!)

6:32 A.M.:   I'm awakened by that squeaky bathroom door and the sound of running water. Oh, yes, I remember. Charlie is going fishing this morning.

He leaves, and I roll over. Try to tune in my dream where it left off. My mind races through a thousand soap-opera plots. No such luck. And it was such a great dream, too.

Sometimes new dreams are better than chewed-over ones, anyway. I just hope my nervous system rejects the unfinished memory.

7:37 A.M.:   I hear breathing. No I don't. I hear breathing again. Do I? Open one eye.

"Mom, are you awake?" whispers nine-year-old Michelle. Her friend Jana is standing in long nightgown by her side.

"Didn't I tell you not to wake me?" I ask.

"I didn't, Mom," she says sincerely, "I didn't say a word until you opened your eye."

Another plot left unfinished. I think there's a conspiracy to keep me from sleeping late on Saturdays. Someday I'm going to sleep for five straight days and force myself to remember all those unfinished stories, especially the really juicy ones.

7:40 A.M.:   It's no use. I get up and tiptoe around the kitchen. Set up breakfast for Michelle and Jana, who spent the night. Laura's girl friend, Marianne, also slept over, but they won't be up for hours, hopefully.

Taped to the refrigerator door I see the sign, "Today I start my diet." My handwriting. My tape. I growl back.

Peek inside refrigerator, and then slam the door. I tell myself, *If only I can hold off a little longer before I eat my egg and grapefruit, maybe I can make it to lunchtime.*

7:41 A.M.:   I eat the egg and grapefruit.

8:04 A.M.: Sit down at my desk. It's Saturday, the golden day of the week. How wonderful. No appointments. Pure silence. I start to work.

8:14 A.M.: Two little faces peek around the doorway. "Hi, Mom; we're not gonna disturb you. We're making chocolate chip cookies and we can't find the nuts."

I find the nuts and shield my eyes from the lovely cookie batter in the bowl. The aroma from the cookies blots out all my concentration.

8:30 A.M.: Two bigger faces appear at the door. It's Laura and Marianne, three hours before schedule. "We couldn't sleep, Mom. The cookies smell so *good.* Can't we just have cookies for breakfast?"

9:07 A.M.: *Keep busy,* I tell myself. *Concentrate on your project.* A vision of a ham and cheese on rye persistently runs through my brain. *Block it out, Marabel,* I tell myself. *At noon, you can only have an egg and watercress anyway, so why torture yourself?*

9:21 A.M.: "Mommeeee!" I hear a plaintive wail from my bathroom. I arrive breathlessly to find two little bodies soaking in the bathtub.

"What's wrong?" I ask. "Are you hurt?"

"Mommy, the bubble bath won't bubble," the apologetic little voice begins. "Do you have any bubble bath?"

I hunt through cabinets and find a new box, *guaranteed* to make bubbles. I dump in a quart.

"Thanks, Mommy. I'm sorry. We didn't mean to disturb you."

"It's okay," I answer, wearily. "Why don't you both stay there and soak for a long time in the bubbles?" Bubbles foam and rise. More bubbles. Some spill over the edge. I hope they don't drown in the stuff. I'll never be able to find them. They love it. I head back to the desk.

10:03 A.M.: Laura and Marianne are making doughnuts in the minifryer and can't find the powdered sugar. I can. I do.

I shield my eyes from the lovely, crisp golden clouds resting on paper towels.

10:42 A.M.: I can resist no longer. Arrange watercress all over the plate, cover it with egg slices. Eat with knife and fork, pretending elegance, already dreaming of dinner.

10:53 A.M.: Michelle hungry again. Explain options. Show and tell leftovers from breakfast. Leftovers rejected. She settles on a banana.

12:03 P.M.: The girls are hungry, again. Take orders for lunch: Michelle and Jana—hot dogs with pickles, chips, and Cokes. Laura and Marianne—cheeseburgers with chips and chocolate shakes. Yours truly—one dip low-cal cottage cheese, hold the chips, hold the shake.

12:40 P.M.: Four heads appear at the doorway of the room. "Mom, there's nothing to do. Will you take us to the pool?" I put on my taxi-driver cap. Quick trip to the pool and back. Turn off meter.

1:20 P.M.: Finally back at the desk. How wonderful. Pure silence, but my motivation is gone. I feel sleepy. *Force yourself to concentrate,* I keep repeating to myself.

2:49 P.M.: The phone rings. It's Laura. "Mom, we want to come home. The lifeguard is driving us crazy. He won't let us do anything."

2:51 P.M.: What's the use? Pick up kids. Drop off girl friends. Return home. Turn off meter.

4:01 P.M.: Collapse. (The only compensation of the day: I'm too tired to eat.)

4:22 P.M.: End of "Collapse period" due to Charlie's noisy lawn mower, taking out Michelle's splinter, and fixing Laura's torn jeans.

6:22 P.M.: Dinner (glorious, delicious dinner!) and cleanup.

9:30 P.M.: Prayer time. Then bedtime. Later, I tiptoe into the girls' rooms. Perfect angels.

I think back over the day. It was all worth it. Or rather, *they* were all worth it. But I do have some constructive ideas for *next* Saturday:

1. Make all-purpose cap acceptable for Saturday wear as cook, waitress, taxi driver, and nurse. Should help avoid quick changes and embarrassing moments if wrong hat is worn to wrong occasion.

2. Install drive-in window for takeout orders.

3. Erect sign in front yard showing number of hamburgers served. Ronald McDonald, here I come!

Painless Pizza

Dijon Steak
Lettuce Wedges with
Avocado Dressing
"Veggie" Pizza
Baked Custard

DIJON STEAK
Serves 4

2 pounds sirloin steak or 4 individual strip steaks
¼ cup Dijon mustard
1 garlic clove, minced

Dash of basil
1 green onion, chopped
½ teaspoon Worcestershire
  sauce

Mix mustard, garlic, basil, onion, and Worcestershire sauce together and spread on both sides of steaks. Broil over hot coals to desired degree of doneness.

LETTUCE WEDGES WITH AVOCADO DRESSING
Serves 4

½ head of lettuce, cut in 4
  wedges
1 ripe avocado, peeled, pitted,
  and mashed
1 cup yogurt

1 tablespoon lemon juice
1 tablespoon soy sauce
Pinch of sugar
Dash of oregano
Dash of Tabasco

Chill lettuce wedges. Combine rest of ingredients and chill.
Serve dressing over wedges on chilled salad plates.

"VEGGIE" PIZZA
Serves 4 generously

1 cup sliced onions
1 garlic clove, minced
2 tablespoons olive oil
2 cups of vegetables in bite size
    pieces such as cauliflower,
    zucchini, green pepper,
    mushrooms, sprouts, alfalfa
    (any combination of these is
    fine)

2 tablespoons tomato paste
1 tablespoon water
Dash of oregano and basil
¼ cup shredded mozzarella
    cheese
¼ cup shredded Monterey Jack
    cheese
2 large pita breads, split and
    toasted (optional)

1. Sauté onions and garlic in olive oil until transparent and tender. Add vegetables, cover, and steam for a few minutes until crisp but tender. Stir in tomato paste, water, oregano, and basil.

2. Divide and spread mixture on split, toasted pita breads, if desired, or spread in buttered pie plate. Sprinkle with cheeses and freeze at this point, or place under broiler until cheese is bubbly. Good with any entrée. Easy to make. Freezes well.

BAKED CUSTARD
Serves 6

3 slightly beaten eggs
¼ cup sugar
2 cups skim milk, scalded

1 teaspoon vanilla
Dash of salt
Nutmeg

1. Beat eggs, sugar, salt, and vanilla with rotary beater. Slowly stir in scalded milk.

2. Strain into 6 custard cups; place in shallow pan of hot water. Sprinkle with nutmeg. Bake at 325° for 35 to 40 minutes. Chill.

Figure Formula

Cottage Cheese and Crab Dip
Tomato Salad
Mushroom Patties
Eggplant Casserole
Strawberry or Spiced Banana Milkshake

COTTAGE CHEESE AND CRAB DIP
Serves 4

1 cup cottage cheese   ⅓ cup crab meat
2 tablespoons milk   2 sprigs fresh dill, minced

Blend all ingredients thoroughly. Serve with crisp crackers or vegetable crudites.

TOMATO SALAD
Serves 4

3 large tomatoes, peeled, and cut   16 mint leaves, chopped
    into small wedges   2 tablespoons chopped fresh dill
1 cup low-fat, plain yogurt   Salt and pepper to taste
1 garlic clove, minced

Mix all ingredients together gently. Chill and serve in small bowls.

MUSHROOM PATTIES
Makes 4 or 5

1½ cups finely chopped fresh
mushrooms (don't use
processor)
2 scallions, chopped (use part of
green, too)
2 eggs, beaten

Salt and pepper to taste
¾ cup seasoned bread crumbs
1 cup grated Monterey Jack or
Swiss cheese
1 tablespoon butter

Mix together and form into small balls (for hors d'oeuvres) or 4 or 5 patties. Refrigerate for 30 minutes. Fry in hot butter on one side, flatten slightly and fry other side.

EGGPLANT CASSEROLE
Serves 8–10
From Ryna and Edie's Shangri-la Spa.

6 tomatoes
¼ cup safflower or sesame oil
1 cup chopped onions
1 cup chopped celery

1 cup chopped green pepper
½ teaspoon summer savory
2 eggplants
1⅓ cups cashew nuts, chopped

1. Skin tomatoes by immersing in boiling water one minute and slipping skins off. Cut into fourths and squeeze each section into large saucepan. Bring tomatoes to boil; then simmer until soft.

2. In frying pan, sauté onions, celery, and green pepper in hot oil until tender. Stir in summer savory. Add this mixture to tomatoes and simmer 45 minutes with cover on.

3. When sauce has cooked, peel and slice eggplants into 1 inch cubes. (Don't cut up ahead of time, because they darken and lose nutrients). Salt and pepper to taste.

4. Lightly oil 13 x 9-inch baking dish. Layer in dish ½ eggplant, ½ sauce, ½ cashews. Repeat layers. Bake at 350° for 1 hour.

STRAWBERRY MILK SHAKE
Serves 1

5 large strawberries, fresh or frozen
½ banana
⅓ cup skim milk

⅓ cup water
1 teaspoon honey
1 Sweet 'N Low packet
4 ice cubes

Place all ingredients in blender and whirl until frothy.

TIP: When strawberries are in season, I freeze the big ones on a cookie sheet, and when frozen, store in plastic freezer bags. Then I can make milk shakes all year long.

SPICED BANANA MILK SHAKE
Serves 1

1 ripe banana
½ cup water
½ cup milk

1 teaspoon honey
¼ teaspoon ground cloves
4 ice cubes

Place all ingredients in blender and whirl until frothy.

Spa Special

Savory Chicken
Health Salad Bowl
Green Goddess Dressing
Shifting Sands Sundae

SAVORY CHICKEN
Serves 6

½ cup Italian dressing, regular
or low calorie
2½ to 3-pound chicken cut into
serving pieces

1¼ cups Bran Chex or crumbled
corn flakes

1. In shallow dish, pour Italian dressing over chicken; cover and marinate at least 1 hour, turning occasionally.
2. Preheat oven to 350°. Coat marinated chicken with crumbs. In foil-lined shallow baking pan, place coated chicken skin side up in a single layer. Bake uncovered without turning for 1 hour or until tender.

HEALTH SALAD BOWL
Serves 6

1 head romaine lettuce
2 cups broccoli flowerets
2 cups cauliflower flowerets
1 cup zucchini or yellow squash
slices
1 cup alfalfa sprouts
1 cup sliced mushrooms

½ cup Swiss cheese, cut in bite-
size strips
½ cup Cheddar cheese, cut in
bite-size strips
½ cup raisins
¾ cup broken walnuts
½ cup sunflower seeds

Wash romaine, pat dry and cut in bite-size strips. Toss with rest of vegetables, and divide evenly among 6 large individual salad bowls. Sprinkle each bowl with cheeses, raisins, nuts and sunflower seeds. Pass bowl of dressing.

GREEN GODDESS DRESSING

⅔ cup mayonnaise
½ cup sour cream
¼ cup chopped parsley
2 tablespoons chopped green
   onions
1½ tablespoons lemon juice

Dash of Worcestershire sauce
1½ tablespoons wine vinegar
Pinch of tarragon
Pinch of chervil
Salt and pepper

Blend all ingredients in electric blender.

SHIFTING SANDS SUNDAE
Serves 2
As I savor each bite of this health sundae, I feel one with the ages, thinking of the maidens who must have whipped this up for the caravan travelers of yore.

1 cup plain yogurt
1 tablespoon honey
½ teaspoon vanilla
¼ teaspoon ground cardamon
   (optional)

¼ cup chopped dates
¼ cup chopped walnuts or
   almonds

Mix all ingredients gently together. Serve in goblets and sprinkle with additional nuts, if desired.

Slim, but Fun

> *Chilled Tomato Soup*
> *Beauty Burgers with Cheese Topping*
> *Garden Salad*
> *Poached Ginger Pears*

CHILLED TOMATO SOUP
Serves 4

4 large tomatoes, peeled and cut into pieces or 3 cups tomato juice
2 cups plain, low-fat yogurt
2 garlic cloves, put through press
2 tablespoons lemon juice
Pinch of sugar
1 teaspoon salt
¼ cup chopped chives or green onions
3 tablespoons chopped fresh dill
¼ cup mint leaves (optional)
Dash of Tabasco
Pinch of marjoram leaves (optional)

Puree all ingredients in blender or food processor. Chill and serve in chilled soup bowls.

BEAUTY BURGERS
Serves 4

1 pound ground beef
1 carrot, chopped fine
1 celery stalk, chopped fine
1 small onion, chopped fine
2 tablespoons parsley, chopped fine
1 teaspoon salt
1 teaspoon Worcestershire sauce
1 egg
1 tablespoon wheat germ

Mix all ingredients together and form into 4 large patties. Broil or pan fry. Top each burger with Cheese Topping, if desired.

CHEESE TOPPING

2 cups (about 8 ounces) Cheddar cheese (sharp), grated
2 tablespoons Dijon mustard
⅛ teaspoon cayenne pepper
¼ teaspoon sugar
¼ cup plain, low-fat yogurt

Beat all ingredients except yogurt until well mixed. Stir in yogurt.

NOTE: This is also good chilled as a dip with crackers or crisp vegetables.

GARDEN SALAD
Serves 4

½ cup diced, peeled cucumber
½ cup diced tomato
¼ cup sliced green onion
¼ cup thinly sliced radishes
¼ cup shredded carrot
½ teaspoon salt
Pinch of cayenne pepper
2 cups low-fat cottage cheese
Red onion or tomato (optional)

Fold vegetables, salt, and cayenne gently into cottage cheese. If desired, serve scoop of cottage-cheese mixture on slices of red onion or tomato.

POACHED GINGER PEARS
Serves 4

3 tablespoons brown sugar
1½ cups unsweetened pineapple juice or orange juice
2 cinnamon sticks
2 teaspoons chopped candied ginger
4 large ripe firm pears, peeled, halved and cored (preferably Anjou)
1 tablespoon chopped almonds (optional)

Place sugar, juice, cinnamon sticks, and ginger in a 1½-quart pan. Bring to a boil. Add pears and simmer uncovered 15 minutes, or until they begin to soften, turning pears after 5 minutes. Refrigerate in syrup overnight. Sprinkle with almonds before serving.

10
International Fair

La Festival
Orient Express
Shalom at Home
South Seas Sensation
Main Street, U.S.A.

Grape Leaves International

Several years ago I planned a mealtime project with an international flavor. I wanted to feature native foods and costumes from a different country every night. I thought this background would help our children to understand better the countries they were studying in geography. At the same time, it would help broaden Charlie's tastes beyond the meat-and-potatoes stage.

The project was launched with "Monday in Mexico." Tacos and refried beans and enchiladas. After school, I told the girls about my plan. I could see their little, creative minds working, as we talked about decorations. They went off to their rooms, and soon emerged with ponchos and sombreros.

I dressed as a senorita with a miniskirt, brightly colored blouse, mesh stockings, and heels, with a red bandana to ward off (or entice) any charging bulls. *Olé!* Charlie loved it.

The next day, we were off to Europe: "Tuesday in Athens." I was anxious to try Greek food, especially baklava, one of my favorite desserts.

I searched the cookbooks until I found a recipe for stuffed grape leaves. It sounded ethnic and exotic. I pictured the Greek mothers of bygone days packing a picnic basket of stuffed grape leaves and baklava for dinner outdoors on the Acropolis lawn.

Charlie even offered to help. He arrived home a little early, so I sent him out with my grocery list. It turned out that grocery shopping was more difficult than he expected. He soon realized that our local supermarket didn't have much of an assortment of grape leaves. So he improvised. Grape leaves, tea leaves, who cares what kind? The important thing is the *leaves.* He ended up rounding up a few assorted leaves from the backyard and insisted on wrapping them around the ground meat I had prepared, according to the recipe.

When it was time to eat, my little girls and I ran to our rooms and donned our costumes of togas. Little Michelle pulled out a king-size sheet from the closet and looked like a Halloween ghost, dragging her six-foot long train behind her. Charlie thought it was "Haunted House Night."

At supper we girls reclined in our togas. Before we ate, I read from the encyclopedia about Greece, her ancient customs and foods. Then we all tasted the "stuffed whatever leaves." I was dubious about the leaves and their smells. Charlie was even more dubious as he began to chew.

After one bite, I very quickly learned one basic rule of Greek cooking: *When the recipe calls for grape leaves, don't substitute!*

The meal was a disaster, but we enjoyed the baklava and closed with very unGreek-like peanut-butter-and-jelly sandwiches, afterwards.

On Wednesday morning, I told a neighbor about my project, and especially the flopped-leaf recipe. She told me, "Oh, you've got to try our favorite family dish, Polish Chicken Paprikash. Just a minute and I'll give you the recipe."

That night when Charlie arrived home, he was drawn to the kitchen by the rather unusual aroma. His three "girls" were dressed in long dresses with aprons and homemade paper hats.

He looked dubious again. "Don't tell me," he said, "let me guess. It's stuffed fox from the Netherlands."

"Nope," I told him. "Close. It's 'Wednesday in Poland!' "

He was a good sport, but later that night he asked for another American PBJ sandwich.

That lesson ended our round-the-world cookouts. We still occasionally experiment, but here are three simple guidelines I keep in mind while cooking an ethnic dish:

1. Cook it correctly. The food may taste a bit strange because it's unfamiliar, so don't experiment for the first time. Otherwise, you won't know if it's the recipe or your variation that went sour.

2. Start with small portions. Until you're used to it, a little bit of a foreign whatever may go a long way.

3. Keep track of your winners, but never repeat a loser or even a partial winner. Alternate and supplement with familiar dishes. If Chinese-suey one night, try hamburgers the next. Or even hamburgers the *same* night!

La Festival

French Onion Soup Gratiné
Chicken Breasts, Mushrooms,
and Grapes with Cream Sauce
Salade Vinaigrette
Parmesan Zucchini
Chocolate Soufflé

FRENCH ONION SOUP GRATINÉ
Serves 6

5 cups thinly sliced Bermuda
  onions (about 5 onions)
¼ tablespoon sugar
1 tablespoon oil or bacon
  drippings
¼ cup sweet butter
1 tablespoon flour
3 10½-ounce cans condensed
  beef or chicken broth,
  undiluted
3 soup cans of water
1 teaspoon salt

Freshly ground black pepper to
  taste
1 teaspoon Worcestershire
  sauce
Dash of nutmeg (optional)
1 clove garlic, minced
2 dozen slices French bread, cut
  very thin and toasted or
  dried in the oven
1½ cups Swiss or Gruyère
  cheese, grated

1. Early in the day, sprinkle onion slices with sugar. Sauté slowly in oil and butter until golden. Sprinkle flour over onions and blend in. Add beef or chicken broth, water, salt, pepper, Worcestershire, nutmeg, and garlic. Cover and simmer gently 45 minutes.

2. Put 4 or 5 slices of bread in each individual 12-ounce oven-proof bowl. Fill bowls halfway with the liquid. This is important as bread will soften and absorb some liquid. Keep adding liquid gradually to the bowls, making sure they are filled evenly to the tops with the liquid. This is very important, as the cheese crust must not sink into the bowl.

3. Sprinkle cheese on top, without pushing it into liquid, about ¼ cup of cheese per bowl. Press the cheese all around the edges of each bowl so that when it melts it sticks to the sides and forms a crust. Place bowls in 400° oven for approximately 35 minutes.

TIP: Save what you don't use tonight for tomorrow. It will be just as delicious. Freezes well, too.

CHICKEN BREASTS, MUSHROOMS, AND GRAPES WITH CREAM SAUCE
Serves 6

3 one-pound chicken breasts, skinned, halved, and boned	¼ pound fresh mushrooms, cut in slices
2 tablespoons plus 1 teaspoon fresh lemon juice	1 cup seedless green grapes (optional)
Salt	1½ tablespoons flour
Freshly ground pepper	1 cup canned chicken stock
3 tablespoons butter	¾ cup heavy cream
2 tablespoons oil	

1. Preheat oven to 450°. With paper towels pat chicken breasts completely dry and rub on both sides with ½ teaspoon lemon juice, a little salt, and few grindings of pepper.

2. In a heavy 12-inch skillet with ovenproof handle, warm 2 tablespoons each of butter and oil over moderate heat for about 10 seconds. Add chicken and sauté until pieces are firm and white, but do not allow to brown. Remove pan from heat and cover tightly with foil. Bake chicken breasts in the middle of the oven for 8 minutes, or until tender.

3. Arrange chicken attractively in an ovenproof casserole or platter and set in oven at 250°. Pour chicken juices into medium skillet, and over moderate heat on top of the stove, add green grapes. Cover and cook 2 minutes. Remove grapes with slotted spoon and put on top of chicken. Add mushrooms and 2 tablespoons lemon juice to skillet and cook 3 minutes. With slotted spoon remove mushrooms and scatter over chicken breasts. Cover tightly with foil and keep chicken warm in oven, while you prepare sauce.

4. With a wire whisk, stir 1 tablespoon butter into liquid re-

maining in skillet. Add flour and continue to whisk until it is completely absorbed. Whisk in chicken stock over high heat until sauce comes to a boil and thickens lightly. Reduce heat to simmer and simmer 8 minutes. Pour cream in slow, thin stream and, stirring frequently, continue to simmer until the sauce is reduced to about 1 cup. Remove from heat and add remaining ½ teaspoon of lemon juice. Taste for seasoning. Pour sauce directly over chicken and serve at once.

SALADE VINAIGRETTE

1 medium head iceberg lettuce, broken up	Salt
	½ cup vinegar
2 carrots, shredded	2 tablespoons prepared mustard
Juice of 1 lemon	6 to 8 fresh mushrooms, wiped
1 cucumber, thinly sliced	clean and sliced

1. Rinse lettuce and dry thoroughly. Squeeze lemon juice over carrots and toss well. Sprinkle cucumbers with salt and let stand 30 to 60 minutes, then rinse well and dry thoroughly.

2. Arrange lettuce on platter and garnish ⅓ of platter with carrots, ⅓ with cucumber, and ⅓ with sliced mushrooms. Dribble on some sauce and serve the rest on the side.

VINAIGRETTE SAUCE

2 tablespoons French Dijon-style mustard	1 egg yolk
	3 shallots, finely chopped
½ cup wine vinegar	1 tablespoon finely chopped
1 teaspoon salt	parsley
⅛ teaspoon pepper	1 clove garlic, finely chopped
1 cup oil	(optional)

1. In a mixing bowl, combine mustard, vinegar, salt, and pepper. Beating with wire whisk or electric mixer, start adding oil in thin stream. Beat constantly until oil is incorporated, making creamy sauce.

2. Beat in egg yolk, shallots, parsley, and garlic. If the dressing seems too thick, add few drops of water to reach desired consistency.

PARMESAN ZUCCHINI
Serves 4

4 to 5 medium zucchini, sliced   1 tablespoon butter
    thin   Salt and pepper
2 tablespoons water   Freshly grated Parmesan cheese

Cook zucchini with butter in water, about 5 minutes. Sprinkle with seasonings and cheese, and serve.

CHOCOLATE SOUFFLÉ
Serves 8
Incredibly delicious.

6 tablespoons butter   1⅓ cups sugar
4 squares unsweetened   6 eggs, separated
    chocolate   ¼ teaspoon salt
½ cup flour   2 teaspoons vanilla
2 cups milk

1. Melt butter with chocolate over low heat. With whisk, blend in flour and salt. Stir in milk and half sugar. Stir and cook over medium heat until thick (about 15 minutes). Stir in beaten egg yolks and vanilla. Set aside to cool. (You may make this early in the day and refrigerate. The beautiful advantage in making a soufflé is that you make the main part ahead of time, and it's a snap to put it together for the oven, just before you sit down to dinner.)

2. Preheat oven to 425°. Oil the insides of 2 1½-quart soufflé dishes, dust lightly with sugar, and refrigerate. (A cold dish makes the soufflé rise.) Reheat chocolate mixture over boiling water until warm, stirring occasionally. Remove from heat.

3. Beat egg whites until fluffy. Gradually add rest of sugar, beating until stiff. Stir ⅓ of whites into chocolate mixture; then fold in rest of whites.

4. Pour into oiled and sugared soufflé dishes. Set in shallow cake pans filled with hot water and bake for 40 minutes. When done, soufflé will wiggle slightly when you move the dish, but

should be high, dark and crusty on outside. Serve with softened vanilla ice cream mixed with a little whipped cream.

TIP: For just our family, I halve the recipe. Everybody gets into the act of whipping the egg whites with a big whisk!

VARIATION for SOUFFLÉ ROLL: This recipe can be used to make a delicate, delectable, cold soufflé roll that absolutely makes your taste buds cry out in ecstasy.
1. Prepare 15 x 11-inch jellyroll pan instead of soufflé dish. Generously grease jellyroll pan, line with sheet of waxed paper with edges hanging over ends about 2 inches. Butter waxed paper generously.
2. Prepare ingredients above and pour into waxed paper in pan. Bake about 15 min. at 350° until puffed and firm and toothpick inserted in "cake" comes out clean.
3. With knife or metal spatula, loosen edges of soufflé. Invert on foil that has been sprinkled with powdered sugar. Peel off waxed paper and cool.
4. Using foil to guide soufflé, roll up carefully in jellyroll fashion. Unroll. Spread with 1 cup sweetened whipped cream and roll up again. Chill several hours.

Orient Express

> *Stir-Fry Chicken with Broccoli*
> *Fluffy Rice*
> *Gingered Melon Balls*

STIR-FRY CHICKEN WITH BROCCOLI
Serves 6

Prepare early in the day and refrigerate. Cooking time takes only a few minutes.

Chicken:

3 whole chicken breasts, boned, skinned and cut into 1 x 1 x ¼ inch strips

¼ cup soy sauce

1 tablespoon cornstarch

2 teaspoons minced, peeled ginger root or ½ teaspoon ground ginger

Sauce:

¼ cup soy sauce

1 teaspoon sugar

1 tablespoon cornstarch

½ cup chicken broth or bouillon

2 teaspoons minced, peeled ginger root or ½ teaspoon ground ginger

To Finish:

4 tablespoons salad oil

¼ cup sliced green onions, including some of green tops

4 cups broccoli flowerets

1 garlic clove, minced (optional)

¾ cup blanched whole almonds, walnuts, or cashew nuts (about 4 ounces)

1. Mix soy sauce, cornstarch, and ginger in bowl. Add chicken and stir to coat thoroughly. Let stand at least 15 minutes.

2. Mix all sauce ingredients in small bowl. Set aside.

3. In wok or large skillet, add nuts to 1 tablespoon hot oil. Cook one minute, or until lightly toasted. Set aside.

4. In 2 tablespoons hot oil, stir fry broccoli for 1 to 2 minutes.

Transfer to large bowl. In remaining 2 tablespoons oil, cook chicken until pieces turn white.

5. Put all ingredients in skillet and cook 30 seconds or until sauce thickens. Serve with hot Fluffy Rice.

VARIATION: Cook in one tablespoon of hot salad oil for 2 minutes, 1 6-ounce package frozen Chinese pea pods, thawed and dried with paper towels. Add 2 tablespoons orange marmalade to chicken mixture.

OTHER POSSIBLE ADDITIONS:

1 8½-ounce can water chestnuts, drained and sliced	**2 green or red sweet peppers, cut in 1-inch squares**
1 8-ounce can bamboo shoots, drained and diced	**½ pound mushrooms, thinly sliced**
¾ cup diced celery	

FLUFFY RICE
Serves 6

1 10¾-ounce can chicken broth, undiluted	**¼ teaspoon salt**
	1 teaspoon butter
1 cup uncooked regular rice	

Mix broth with water to equal 2 cups. Combine with rice and salt in saucepan. Bring to boil, stir once, cover tightly and simmer 15 minutes. Let rice set covered for 5 minutes. Add butter, stir lightly, and serve.

GINGERED MELON BALLS
Serves 6

3 cups watermelon balls	**3 teaspoons orange juice**
2 cups honeydew balls	**1 teaspoon brown sugar**
1 cup green grapes, cut in half (optional)	**2 teaspoons chopped crystalized ginger**
2 teaspoons lemon juice	

Mix all ingredients gently together. Refrigerate 1 hour. Serve in small shallow bowls.

Shalom at Home

Party Dip with Vegetable Sticks
Mushroom Quiche
Mediterranean Salad
Spice Crumb Cake

PARTY DIP WITH VEGETABLE STICKS

1 cup mayonnaise
¼ cup finely chopped green
  onions
¼ cup finely chopped green
  pepper
¼ cup bottled chili sauce
2 teaspoons chopped parsley
¼ teaspoon salt

Dash of pepper
1 tablespoon lemon juice
¼ cup heavy cream, whipped
Cut fresh vegetables: crisp green
  peppers, sweet red peppers,
  carrots, scallions, mushrooms, zucchini, broccoli,
  and cauliflower flowerets

Lightly mix all ingredients except vegetables together. For variation, omit green pepper and chili sauce, and add 1 teaspoon chopped fresh dill and one teaspoon Dijon mustard.

MUSHROOM QUICHE
Serves 6 as main dish
Delicate and delicious!

1 9-inch unbaked pie shell
5 tablespoons butter
1 pound fresh mushrooms, sliced
1 teaspoon lemon juice
½ teaspoon salt
½ lb. Gruyère cheese, grated
  (about 2 cups)
4 eggs
1½ cups whipping cream or light
  cream

¼ teaspoon freshly ground
  pepper
Few drops of Tabasco
  (optional)
Dash of nutmeg
½ cup Parmesan cheese, grated
  (optional)

1. Preheat oven to 350°. Sauté sliced mushrooms in butter with salt and lemon juice until mushrooms are soft and all liquid has evaporated. Mix mushroom mixture gently with Gruyère cheese. Spoon into pie shell.
2. Beat eggs; add cream, salt, pepper, Tabasco sauce, and nutmeg. Pour over mushrooms and cheese. Sprinkle Parmesan cheese on top if desired. Bake 40 to 45 minutes or until puffed and golden. Allow to stand 10 to 15 minutes before serving.

MEDITERRANEAN SALAD
Serves 6

1 medium cucumber, sliced	Dash of oregano
2 large tomatoes, cut in eighths	1 tablespoon chopped parsley
6 ounces Feta cheese	½ teaspoon dried basil leaves
1 cup Greek olives	½ teaspoon dried thyme leaves
¼ cup olive oil	⅛ teaspoon pepper
2 tablespoons wine vinegar	6 large lettuce leaves
3 tablespoons thinly sliced green onions	Anchovy fillets (optional)

Crumble cheese into salad bowl. Add cucumbers, tomatoes, and olives. In small jar with tight-fitting lid combine olive oil, vinegar, green onions, oregano, parsley, basil, thyme leaves, and pepper. Shake until well blended. Pour over cheese and vegetables. Toss gently. Serve on lettuce leaves. Garnish with anchovies on top.

SPICE CRUMB CAKE

3 cups sifted flour	1½ teaspoons ground nutmeg
2¼ cups (1-pound box) firmly packed, light brown sugar	½ teaspoon cinnamon
¾ cup butter	¾ cup chopped pecans or walnuts
1 cup sour cream	1 teaspoon vanilla
1½ teaspoons baking soda	½ cup shredded coconut
2 eggs	

1. Preheat oven to 350°. Grease and flour a 13 x 9 x 2-inch baking pan. Mix flour, brown sugar, and butter with pastry blender until crumbly. Reserve ¾ cup of the mixture. Combine sour cream and soda. Stir eggs, spices, vanilla, and sour-cream-and-soda mixture into crumb mixture.

2. Pour batter into prepared pan; sprinkle with coconut and nuts, and reserved ¾ cup crumb mixture. Bake in 350° oven for 40 to 45 minutes or until done.

South Seas Sensation

Spicy Roast Pork
Wild Rice Casserole
Stir-fried Vegetables
Brown Sugar Rolls
Fiji Chocolate Meringue Pie

SPICY ROAST PORK
Serves 6–8

1 3-pound boned pork loin
1 garlic clove, cut in half
2 cups sugar
1 cup water
1 cup vinegar
2 tablespoons chopped green
 pepper
1 teaspoon dry mustard

1 teaspoon soy sauce
1 teaspoon salt
½ teaspoon pepper
4 teaspoons cornstarch
2 tablespoons water
2 teaspoons paprika
2 tablespoons finely chopped
 parsley

1. Preheat oven to 450°. Rub pork loin all over with cut ends of garlic. Roast in shallow pan 30 minutes or until brown. Mix sugar, water, vinegar, green pepper, mustard, soy sauce, salt, and pepper in saucepan and boil gently for 5 minutes.

2. Mix cornstarch with 2 tablespoons water to make smooth paste. Add to sugar mixture and cook over low heat, stirring until thickened. Strain through sieve. Add paprika and parsley. Pour sauce over pork, lower oven to 300° and bake 2 hours longer, or until meat thermometer registers 180–185°. Serve on warm platter with sauce in warm gravy boat. Garnish with watercress.

WILD RICE CASSEROLE
Serves 8

4 tablespoons butter
1 cup wild rice
½ cup slivered almonds
2 tablespoons green onions or chives
1 teaspoon soy sauce

1 5-ounce can water chestnuts, sliced
3 4-ounce cans mushrooms, drained
3 cups hot chicken broth

1. Preheat oven to 350°. Put all ingredients except broth in heavy frying pan. Cook over medium-high heat 20 minutes, or until almonds are slightly brown. Stir often.

2. Add hot chicken broth; stir. Pour into 2-quart baking dish. Cover tightly with foil. Bake 2 hours.

STIR-FRIED VEGETABLES
Serves 8

1 tablespoon peanut or vegetable oil
½ cup carrots, slivered
½ cup celery, slivered
2 medium zucchini, sliced thinly on the bias

2 tablespoons chicken broth or water
¼ pound snow peas
Salt and pepper to taste

1. Heat oil in skillet until very hot. Add carrots and stir-fry one minute. Add celery and zucchini and stir one minute more.

2. Add chicken broth or water and cover. Cook 30 seconds. Add snow peas, cover, and cook 30 seconds more. Season with salt and pepper, stir, and serve at once.

BROWN SUGAR ROLLS
Makes 8 rolls

1 package crescent rolls
8 marshmallows

Brown sugar
3 tablespoons butter, melted

Roll each marshmallow in butter, then in sugar. Wrap crescent triangle around coated marshmallow, sealing edges *tightly.* Dip top of roll in melted butter and then in sugar. Place sugar side up on ungreased cookie sheet. Bake in preheated oven at 375° for 12 minutes.

FIJI CHOCOLATE MERINGUE PIE
Serves 6–8

4 egg whites
Dash of salt
⅔ cup sugar
1 cup chopped nuts
1 tablespoon powdered instant coffee

2 teaspoons vanilla
1 cup whipping cream
1 6-ounce package semisweet chocolate chips
⅔ cup sweetened condensed milk
2 tablespoons butter

1. Early in the day or day before, beat egg whites and salt until soft peaks form. Add sugar slowly, beating until stiff peaks form. Fold in nuts.

2. Preheat oven to 275°. Spread in buttered 9-inch pie plate forming a high edge on sides. Bake in oven for one hour. Turn off oven and let meringue shell cool in oven with door closed for 2 hours.

3. Combine instant coffee, vanilla, and whipping cream in medium bowl and chill while you make rest of pie. Also chill your eggbeater.

4. Add chocolate chips to sweetened condensed milk and cook in double boiler over rapidly boiling water until thickened, about 8 minutes. Stir in butter and cool.

5. Whip cream mixture with chilled eggbeater until thick. Fold this mixture into chocolate mixture. Pour into meringue crust. Cover with plastic wrap and freeze 6 hours or overnight. If you have too much mixture for pie shell, chill excess and mound on pie after it is frozen.

Main Street, U.S.A.

> *New England Clam Chowder*
> *Glazed Ham*
> *Orange-Glazed Sweet Potatoes*
> *Dixie Green Beans*
> *Corn Scallop*
> *Old-Fashioned Strawberry Shortcake*

NEW ENGLAND CLAM CHOWDER
Makes 8 cups

2 cups canned clams, drained and chopped
1 large boiled potato, diced
½ cup chopped onion
1 green pepper, chopped
4 slices bacon, fried and crumbled
1½ teaspoons bacon drippings
2½ cups hot milk
1½ tablespoons flour
2 cups clam juice
3 cups chicken stock or broth
1½ teaspoons Worcestershire sauce
¼ teaspoon Tabasco
1 teaspoon salt
¼ teaspoon pepper

1. Sauté onion and green pepper in bacon drippings. Blend in flour with wire whisk; stir in hot milk. Cook and stir until slightly thickened.

2. Stir in rest of ingredients, except clams. Heat but do not boil. Add clams and remove from heat. Serve in mugs.

GLAZED HAM
Serves 12

5 pound canned ham
1 10-ounce jar orange marmalade
1 tablespoon prepared mustard
½ cup orange juice
Dash of cloves
Dash of ginger
Whole cloves

1. Preheat oven to 325 °. Score fat on ham, place in baking pan. Bake 1 hour.
2. Mix rest of ingredients in small saucepan and simmer 5 minutes. Stud ham with whole cloves and spoon half of glaze over ham. Bake 30 minutes more. Spoon rest of glaze over ham. Bake 10 minutes more.

ORANGE-GLAZED SWEET POTATOES
Serves 4

½ of a 3-ounce package orange-flavored gelatin
2½ tablespoons brown sugar
½ cup boiling water
Dash of salt

2 tablespoons butter
1 17-ounce can vacuum-packed sweet potatoes, drained
Dash of allspice (optional)

In large skillet, dissolve gelatin, brown sugar, and salt in boiling water. Add butter and bring to boiling, stirring constantly. Add sweet potatoes; sprinkle with allspice and simmer, basting frequently, till syrup thickens and potatoes are glazed, about 15 minutes.

DIXIE GREEN BEANS
Serves 8

2 packages frozen French-style green beans
4 teaspoons butter, softened
1 tablespoon lemon juice

4 tablespoons chopped toasted almonds
2 teaspoons Dijon mustard

Cook beans according to directions on box. Drain. Combine rest of ingredients; add to beans and toss gently.

CORN SCALLOP
Serves 8

1 8-ounce can cream-style corn
1 8-ounce can whole kernel corn
1 stick butter, melted
1 cup sour cream
1 8½-ounce package corn muffin
   mix

Drop or two of Tabasco
   (optional)
2 eggs, beaten slightly
1 4-ounce can green chilies,
   chopped (optional)

Do not drain corn. Mix all ingredients together thoroughly. Bake at 350° for 35 to 40 minutes in soufflé dish or 11 x 7-inch baking dish. Puffs up and gets a crusty top.

OLD-FASHIONED STRAWBERRY SHORTCAKE
Serves 8

3 cups sliced strawberries
2 cups flour
¼ cup sugar
Dash of nutmeg
4 teaspoons baking powder
1 teaspoon salt

½ cup butter or vegetable
   shortening
⅔ cup milk
1 cup heavy cream, whipped and
   sweetened with 1 teaspoon
   of powdered sugar

1. Preheat oven to 425°. Sweeten berries with 2 tablespoons sugar. Refrigerate.

2. Mix dry ingredients together. Blend in butter or vegetable shortening with pastry blender until mixture is mealy. Add milk and stir just until mixed. Batter will not be smooth. Form 8 mounds on greased cookie sheet or spoon batter into *well-buttered* 8-inch layer cake pan.

3. Bake mounds 10 to 12 minutes or cake 12 to 15 minutes or until it tests done with a toothpick. Cool on rack.

4. To serve, split cake, butter lower layer, cover with half the berries, top with 2nd layer. Add rest of berries and whipped cream on top.

11
Unexpected Dinner Guests

Ready, Already
Spur of the Moment
Clark Kent's Telephone Booth
Company Insurance

The Rise and Fall of the Company Soufflé

One afternoon when I was a brand-new bride, Charlie called from law school to say, "You'll never guess what happened! I just ran into my old college roommate. He's in town with two friends and I invited all of them home for dinner. Don't go to any trouble. Just be casual. See you at six. Bye."

I hung up the phone, stunned. Married only two months, and my husband was true to form, bringing home the proverbial guests!

"Don't go to any trouble." (*Of course not. Only three extra people. Men. Hungry men. And besides, how do I know what they like?*).

I looked at the clock. I looked in the mirror. I looked around the room. Total disaster everywhere. Less than three hours to grocery shop, (on a very meager budget), cook and set up, clean the apartment, and then get myself "gussied up."

But instead of worrying, I told myself, *I'm going to do it*. And I did. I accomplished more in that next hour than I had the previous three weeks. I made it through that global crisis. It's true the chicken à la king was a little soggy, but then so was I.

Since then I have learned a lot about surprise dinners, mostly out of necessity. But it still never comes easy to me. Whenever I hear that Aunt Agnes is arriving on the 6:10, trauma again whips through my heart, until I remember that my shelves are stocked for just such an emergency with tins of tuna and chicken, and even a full-course dinner in the freezer.

As philosopher Henry Drummond once said, "The greatest thing a man can do for his heavenly Father is to be kind to some of His other children." Even if they do drop in unexpectedly, I might add.

Ready, Already

"Mini" Franks in Sweet-and-Sour Sauce
Chicken Divan
Cherry Tomatoes with Garlic
Sautéed Peaches or Bananas
Cherry Crunch

"MINI" FRANKS IN SWEET-AND-SOUR SAUCE
Serves 6–8
A five-minute appetizer!

2 teaspoons currant jelly
2 teaspoons prepared mustard

Can or package of small wieners
or cocktail franks

Heat jelly and mustard, stirring to blend. Simmer a few minutes. Serve surrounded with heated franks and toothpicks for dunking.

TIP: I keep a batch of this super sauce stored in the freezer. The proportions are 6 ounces prepared mustard and 1 10-ounce jar currant jelly. Simmer 25 minutes. Freeze.

CHICKEN DIVAN
Serves 6 generously

10 to 12 slices of cooked chicken breasts or 5 5-ounce cans boned chicken
2 packages frozen broccoli spears, cooked according to package directions

2 teaspoons Worcestershire sauce
1 tablespoon lemon juice
½ teaspoon curry powder (optional)
1 cup mayonnaise

2 10½-ounce cans cream of   6 ounces sharp Cheddar or Swiss
chicken soup, undiluted   cheese, grated
Dash of cayenne pepper

TOPPING

3 ounces grated cheese   ¼ cup sliced almonds (optional)
½ cup buttered bread crumbs

1. Preheat oven to 350°. In buttered 9 x 13-inch baking dish, place drained broccoli spears; layer chicken slices on top.
2. Combine remaining ingredients and cover chicken and broccoli. Bake 30 minutes. Sprinkle with topping. Bake 10 more minutes. This dish can be prepared early in day and baked just before serving.

VARIATION: In place of broccoli, use 2 14½-ounce cans asparagus spears, drained.

CHERRY TOMATOES WITH GARLIC
Serves 6

24 ripe cherry tomatoes   3 tablespoons butter
Boiling water   ¼ teaspoon freshly ground
1 teaspoon salt   pepper
1 clove garlic or more, crushed in   ¼ cup chopped parsley
**   press**

1. Place tomatoes in a wire sieve; dip in rapidly boiling water for about 10 seconds, or until skins loosen. Remove skins and sprinkle tomatoes with salt; let stand 15 minutes.
2. Preheat oven to 350°. Melt butter in shallow ovenproof dish. Add garlic and pepper; add drained tomatoes, shaking to coat with mixture. Place in oven just long enough to heat through (1 to 2 minutes). Be careful not to overcook. Sprinkle with parsley and serve immediately.

SAUTÉED PEACHES OR BANANAS
Serves 6

4 tablespoons butter
4 peaches or bananas, peeled (or
a mixture of both)

2 tablespoons light brown sugar
1 teaspoon cinnamon

1. Melt butter in skillet. Add peach halves or split bananas and sauté on both sides until golden. (Even peaches that are not juicy or quite ripe taste good in this recipe.)
2. Mix sugar and cinnamon and sprinkle over both sides of fruit. Cook a little longer until sugar begins to caramelize.

CHERRY CRUNCH
Serves 6
Takes 5 minutes to put together

1 can cherry pie filling (any fruit
filling is great)
1 small can crushed pineapple,
drained (optional)
1 small cake mix (white or yel-
low Jiffy or ½ of a large
mix)

2 tablespoons brown sugar
¾ cup oatmeal, either quick or
regular
¼ teaspoon cinnamon
½ cup chopped nuts or coconut
(optional)
6 tablespoons butter, melted

1. Spread pie filling and pineapple in 9-inch square baking dish.
2. Mix cake mix, sugar, oatmeal, cinnamon and nuts or coconut. Sprinkle over pie filling. Pour melted butter over top. Bake for one hour at 350°. Serve warm with ice cream.

Spur of the Moment

Spicy Tomato Juice
Baked Chicken and Wild Rice
Hot Garlic Bread
Scrumptious Spinach
Easy Mocha Mousse

SPICY TOMATO JUICE
Serves 8

1 46-ounce can tomato or V-8
  juice
½ of a 12-ounce bottle chili
  sauce

Dash of Tabasco
2 teaspoons Worcestershire
  sauce
Pinch of oregano

Mix together. Chill. Serve in chilled goblets or glasses with lemon wedges.

BAKED CHICKEN AND WILD RICE
Serves 8

5 chicken breasts, cut in half, or
  10 thighs
1 10½-ounce can cream of celery
  soup
1 10½-ounce can cream of mushroom soup
1 cup wild and long-grain rice,
  uncooked

1 4-ounce can mushroom bits or
  ½ pound fresh mushrooms
  sautéed in 2 tablespoons
  butter
1 package dry onion-soup
  mix
1 8-ounce can water chestnuts,
  drained and sliced

Preheat oven to 325°. In a 13 x 9-inch baking dish, mix all ingredients, except chicken, together. Lay chicken on top, skin side
up. Cover with aluminum foil. Bake 2 hours. Don't look! Remove
foil, brush chicken with butter, and continue baking about 15 minutes more to brown.

HOT GARLIC BREAD
Serves 8

½ cup butter
2 cloves garlic, minced
1 teaspoon marjoram or basil
   leaves, crushed

¼ teaspoon pepper
2 tablespoons parsley, chopped
1 Italian or Vienna bread loaf

Blend butter, garlic and spices. At 1-inch intervals, cut bread in
diagonal slices nearly through to bottom. Butter slices on one side
only with garlic mixture. Bake bread, wrapped in foil, in 375° oven
for 15 to 20 minutes.

SCRUMPTIOUS SPINACH
Serves 6–8

2 packages frozen chopped spinach, cooked and drained
   well
½ cup mayonnaise

½ cup sour cream
½ package dry onion-soup mix
Parmesan cheese (optional)
Few slivered almonds (optional)

Mix together spinach, mayonnaise, sour cream, and onion soup
mix. Spoon into buttered casserole. Sprinkle with Parmesan cheese
and almonds, if desired. Heat in preheated 325° oven for 35
minutes.

EASY MOCHA MOUSSE
Serves 6–8

1½ cups semisweet chocolate pieces
⅓ cup hot coffee
Dash of cinnamon (optional)
1 teaspoon vanilla

4 egg yolks
4 egg whites, at room temperature
3 tablespoons brown sugar
½ cup whipped cream (optional)

1. Blend chocolate pieces, coffee, and cinnamon in blender for 30 seconds. Add yolks and vanilla, and blend 30 seconds.

2. In large bowl, beat egg whites until fluffy. Slowly beat in sugar until stiff. Fold whites into chocolate mixture.

3. Spoon into serving bowl or small parfait glasses. Chill at least 1 hour, preferably 2. Garnish with whipped cream, if desired.

Clark Kent's Telephone Booth

> Crab Mousse Appetizer
> Baked Chicken Larghetto
> Fettucini
> Piquant Tomatoes
> Raspberry Ice-Cream Sundaes

CRAB MOUSSE APPETIZER
Serves 8
A luscious spread for crackers.

1 10¾-ounce can cream of mushroom soup
1½ envelopes plain gelatin
3 tablespoons cold water
1 cup mayonnaise
1 teaspoon Worcestershire sauce
1 jar pimento, drained and chopped (optional)

8 ounces cream cheese at room temperature
1 cup finely chopped celery
1 cup finely chopped onion
12 ounces crab meat, fresh or frozen (chopped lobster may be substituted)
6 drops Tabasco

1. Dissolve gelatin in cold water. Warm undiluted soup over low heat, and add gelatin, stirring until completely dissolved. With wire whisk, stir in rest of ingredients.

2. Pour in fish mold and chill several hours until firm. Unmold on pretty plate. Surround with crackers.

BAKED CHICKEN LARGHETTO
Serves 8

2 3-pound chickens, cut in
    pieces
½ cup flour
2 sticks butter, melted

1½ teaspoon dry mustard
Paprika
Pepper
Seasoned or regular salt

1. Put flour and chicken pieces (a few at a time) in paper bag and shake to coat chicken.

2. Stir mustard and butter together in shallow bowl or pie plate. Dip flour-coated chicken pieces in butter and lay skin side up on foil-lined cookie sheet (one which has a rim). Sprinkle with paprika, pepper, and salt. Bake uncovered 1 hour at 400°.

FETTUCINI
Serves 6

¼ cup butter
4 eggs
¼ cup whipping cream
8 ounces bacon, cut up (optional)
1 pound fettucini or linguine
    noodles

½ to 1 cup freshly grated Parmesan cheese
2 tablespoons chopped parsley
¼ teaspoon freshly ground
    pepper

1. Let butter, eggs, and cream stand at room temperature. Fry bacon until crisp and drain on paper towels.

2. Cook fettucini according to box directions, in boiling salted water to which 1 tablespoon oil has been added (about 15 minutes).

3. Beat eggs and cream together until just blended. Drain fettucini in colander, but do not rinse, and return pasta to the still hot pot.

4. Toss pasta with butter. Add cream mixture and toss until well coated. Add rest of ingredients and toss. Sprinkle lightly with salt and serve immediately. Delicious the next day, too.

VARIATION: You may prepare this ahead of time. Spread combined ingredients in buttered 12 x 8-inch baking dish and sprinkle with ½ cup seasoned bread crumbs. Bake at 350° for 10 to 15 minutes to heat through.

PIQUANT TOMATOES
Serves 8

4 tomatoes, sliced
⅓ cup salad oil
½ cup vinegar
2 tablespoons chopped fresh
  parsley
2 tablespoons chopped green
  onions

⅛ teaspoon pepper
½ teaspoon thyme
1 clove garlic, crushed in press
1½ tablespoons sugar
½ teaspoon salt
8 lettuce leaves (optional)

1. Arrange tomatoes in dish. Mix remaining ingredients except lettuce leaves, and pour over tomatoes. Cover with plastic wrap and refrigerate several hours.

2. Serve several slices tomatoes atop lettuce leaf on individual salad plates. Spoon dressing over top.

RASPBERRY ICE-CREAM SUNDAES
Serves 6

1 10-ounce package frozen rasp-
  berries, thawed

1 teaspoon cornstarch
1 quart vanilla ice cream

1. Drain ⅔ cup juice from thawed raspberries, set berries aside. Stir juice and cornstarch in small pan; mix well. Stir over medium heat and boil 1 minute. Cool; then refrigerate. When cold, mix gently with raspberries.

2. To serve, put scoops of ice cream in tall goblets. Spoon raspberry sauce on top. Stick sprig of fresh mint or garnish with whipped cream on top.

Company Insurance

ASPARAGUS SOUP
Serves 6

3 tablespoons butter
2 tablespoons flour
1½ cups milk
1 cup chicken broth
1 14½-ounce can green asparagus (juice and all, pureed)

¼ teaspoon salt
⅛ teaspoon pepper
2 tablespoons chopped parsley
Whipped cream (optional)
Dash of mace (optional)

1. In saucepan over low heat, melt butter. Add flour and blend until smooth.
2. Add milk and broth and cook 10 minutes.
3. Add asparagus, mix and heat to boiling. Add salt, pepper, and parsley.

PARTY CHICKEN BREASTS
Serves 8

4 whole chicken breasts, boned, skinned, and split
8 bacon slices, slightly cooked and blotted on paper towels
1 5-ounce package dried beef
1 10¾-ounce can cream of mushroom soup, undiluted

1 cup sour cream or mayonnaise
1 cup fresh mushrooms, sliced (optional)
2 tablespoons apple juice (optional)

1. Preheat oven to 300°. Wrap slice of bacon around each breast. Arrange beef in bottom of 9 x 13-inch buttered baking dish. Place chicken on top in single layer. Mix soup, sour cream, mushrooms, and apple juice. Spread over chicken, covering well.

2. Bake uncovered in 300° oven for 2 hours, or in 350° oven for 1½ hours.

ZUCCHINI STUFFING CASSEROLE
Serves 6–8

¼ cup butter
2 carrots, grated
1 large onion, chopped
2½ cups stuffing mix
1 10¾-ounce can cream of mushroom or chicken soup

½ cup sour cream
4 medium zucchini, sliced in ½-inch thick pieces
2 tablespoons butter, melted

1. Preheat oven to 350°. In melted butter, sauté carrots and onion until tender. Stir in 2 cups stuffing mix, soup, and sour cream. Remove from heat.

2. Cook zucchini in boiling salted water a few minutes, just until tender. Add to vegetable mixture. Pour into buttered casserole dish. Mix remaining ½ cup of stuffing mix with 2 tablespoons melted butter and sprinkle on top. Bake for 30 minutes.

LETTUCE WITH CREAMY DRESSING
Serves 8

1 head lettuce, cut into 8 wedges
½ cup mayonnaise
2 tablespoons chopped onion
1 tablespoon white vinegar
⅛ teaspoon salt

Dash freshly ground pepper
½ clove garlic minced (optional)
1 teaspoon sugar
¼ teaspoon Italian seasoning

Blend all ingredients except lettuce in blender until smooth. Arrange wedges on individual chilled salad plates. Spoon dressing over top.

ORANGE ICE
Serves 6
Very easy and pretty!

3 oranges   **1 pint orange sherbert**

1. Cut oranges in half and scoop out fruit and membrane. (Save fruit for another purpose.) Fill each half with orange sherbert, mounding nicely. Put in freezer until serving time.

2. Serve each half on leaf-covered dessert plates. (Send children outside to find pretty, large leaves). Tuck sprig of mint or candied violet on top of sherbert.

NOTE: Lemons and lemon sherbert may be substituted. Arranged on a silver tray lined with dark green leaves, these are perfect for a ladies' luncheon, too.

12
Family Outings

Shake Spears
Patio Picnic
Summer Serendipity
Light Fantastic
Private-Office Rendezvous (Dietetic!)

Picnic Panic

Charlie hates picnics. This came as a great blow to me shortly after we were married. While we were dating, I had a dream that our married life would be one, long, continuous picnic. I could see us relaxing amid romantic, pastoral meadows, with happy little children chasing butterflies and an overflowing basket of goodies nearby.

But Charlie didn't appreciate my butterflies. To him *picnic* was spelled i-n-c-o-n-v-e-n-i-e-n-c-e. ("Why forego all the lovely luxuries at home? If you've got an electric can opener, use it!") And picnics also meant extra, annoying work—lots of it. In fact, four stages of it.

Stage one—"The Loading": Picnics require packing the car with hot baked beans, iced cold drinks, little tots, diaper bag, toys, jackets, blankets, pillows, potato chips, bug spray, mustard, napkins, cookies, and relish.

Stage two—"The Unloading": Upon arrival at the park, it's time to unload the cold baked beans, warm drinks, soggy diaper bag, and so on. And then there's the spilled soda and potato chips that slid down the back seat.

Stage three—"The Loading": Getting packed to leave the picnic site always seems fraught with its own particular problems. The kids are tired, the weather is hot, everyone's dusty, sandy, and smelly. The car may be a little bit lighter perhaps, but also much messier. I'll spare you the mystery of the mustard stains in our glove compartment.

Stage four—"The Unloading": Back home, Charlie unpacks all the "grunkle" for the final time, and despairingly transports everything back inside the house. Then it's back outside to clean up the car.

I suppose it's understandable why he considers picnics a sinister experience. Still I love them, but I have changed my strategy. Here are some reminders I keep in mind.

1. Don't announce a picnic in advance. I don't make such a project of picnics anymore. Really, they're often far more successful when thrown together at the last minute.

2. The shorter the travel distance, the better the picnic. Some of

the happiest outings for the Morgan family were simply held in the backyard, where much of the aggravation of loading is eliminated.

3. Plan your strategy like a three-stage rocket. Instead of a three-minute, whirlwind demolition of two dozen hot dogs, a pot of beans, and fourteen deviled eggs, serve the meal in two or more stages. I start with a salad, and then the main course. In between these, and before dessert, they all run wild. So long as I've food remaining, I know they'll be back. And they'll relish that food so much more when they finally do sit down to eat, again.

Shake Spears

Grilled Shish Kebobs
Mexican Rice Ring
Garlic Olives
Lettuce Wedges with Salad Dressings
Picnic Chocolate Cake with Chocolate
or Caramel Frosting
Green and Black Grapes

GRILLED SHISH KEBOBS
Serves 6

2½ pounds beef (or lamb) cut in 2-inch squares

12 cherry tomatoes

12 mushrooms (medium size)

1 6-ounce jar marinated artichoke hearts (optional)

12 small onions or 3 large ones cut in fourths

2 green peppers cut in 1-inch squares

12 bacon squares (optional)

2 or 3 yellow squash, cut in slices

1 or 2 zucchini, cut in slices

Marinate beef squares in marinade for several hours or all day. At serving time, arrange meat and vegetables on skewers, brush with marinade, and broil over hot coals 15 minutes or until cooked. Turn skewers and brush with marinade during the cooking process.

MARINADE FOR SHISH KEBOBS

⅓ cup soy sauce

¾ cup salad oil

⅛ cup Worcestershire sauce

1 tablespoon dry mustard

2 teaspoons salt

1 teaspoon parsley flakes

1½ teaspoons ground pepper

¼ cup wine vinegar

1 garlic clove, crushed, (optional)

¼ cup fresh lemon juice

Blend all ingredients together in blender for half a minute. Pour in jar with tight lid. Refrigerate. Use as desired.

TIP: This marinade is especially tasty on flank steak.

MEXICAN RICE RING
Serves 12

1½ cups converted rice
1½ teaspoons salt
1 cup chopped onion
2 4-ounce cans peeled green chili peppers, drained and chopped, or
½ 4-ounce can *hot* chili peppers chopped

2 cups Monterey Jack or Cheddar cheese, shredded
1 teaspoon salt
½ teaspoon pepper
2 cups sour cream
1 pimento, cut in thin strips (optional)

1. Preheat oven to 350°. In large sauce pot, bring 3¾ cups water to boiling. Stir in rice and salt. Cover tightly and cook over low heat until water is absorbed, about 25 minutes.
2. Sauté onion in butter until soft. Mix with rice, chili peppers, cheese, salt, and pepper in large bowl; toss lightly to mix. Fold in sour cream.
3. Spoon into buttered 8-cup ring mold, packing mixture down lightly with back of spoon. Bake 30 minutes, or until set.
4. Cool in mold on wire rack for 5 minutes. Loosen around edge and center ring with knife; cover with serving plate. Turn upside down; gently lift off mold. Place pimento strips over top of ring. Serve hot or cold.

VARIATION: You may use a casserole dish instead of ring mold. Follow steps 1 and 2 and add 1 cup cream-style cottage cheese. Bake 30 minutes, or until set.

NOTE: May be prepared ahead of time. Also freezes well.

GARLIC OLIVES
Makes 2½ cups

1 7-ounce jar pitted green
   olives, drained
1 7-ounce jar pitted ripe olives,
   drained
1 tablespoon chopped parsley

1 clove garlic, crushed
3 tablespoons olive oil
¼ teaspoon salt
Dash of pepper

In medium bowl, combine all ingredients; toss until well blended. Refrigerate, covered, several days, to develop flavor.

LETTUCE WEDGES WITH SALAD DRESSINGS

Arrange each lettuce wedge on an attractive salad plate and pass dressings. Serve them from red or green peppers which have had the stems removed and are seeded.

RUSSIAN DRESSING

1 cup mayonnaise
½ cup chili sauce
2 tablespoons salad oil

2 teaspoons lemon juice
2 tablespoons sweet pickle relish
1 small onion, finely chopped

Mix all ingredients together. Chill.

BLUE-CHEESE DRESSING

½ cup crumbled Blue cheese
1¼ cups mayonnaise
2 tablespoons light cream
1 teaspoon Worcestershire
   sauce

¼ teaspoon salt
Dash of garlic powder
Dash of white pepper

Mix all ingredients together. Chill.

GARLIC DRESSING

½ cup mayonnaise   ¼ teaspoon oregano
½ cup salad oil   Dash of Worcestershire sauce
¼ cup half-and-half or cream   Salt and pepper to taste
1 garlic clove, minced

Beat salad oil into mayonnaise, a few drops at a time. Stir in rest of ingredients. Chill.

PICNIC CHOCOLATE CAKE
Serves 12

4 squares unsweetened   ¼ teaspoon salt
   chocolate   1½ teaspoons baking soda
1 stick butter   1 cup sour cream
1 cup hot water   2 teaspoons vanilla
2 cups flour   2 eggs beaten
2 cups sugar
½ teaspoon instant coffee powder (optional)

1. Preheat oven to 350°. Butter 13 x 9 x 2-inch baking pan. Melt chocolate squares over hot water. Melt butter in cup of hot water and bring to boil. Combine melted chocolate, butter, and water. Set aside.

2. Sift flour, sugar, coffee powder, and salt together. Add chocolate mixture to flour mixture all at once and blend well.

3. Stir baking soda into sour cream and add to batter. Stir in vanilla and eggs.

4. Bake 30 minutes or until no imprint remains on cake when lightly pressed. While cake is baking, make Chocolate or Caramel frosting.

CHOCOLATE FROSTING

3 squares unsweetened
   chocolate
5 tablespoons milk
3 cups sifted powdered sugar
Dash of salt

1 tablespoon vanilla
5 tablespoons butter, melted
1 teaspoon instant coffee
Dash of cinnamon

Melt chocolate over hot water. Mix milk with powdered sugar and coffee. Add salt, vanilla, and cinnamon. Stir in melted chocolate and butter. Spread on warm cake.

CARAMEL FROSTING

½ cup butter
1 cup light brown sugar
⅓ cup light cream

2 cups unsifted powdered sugar
2 teaspoons vanilla extract

1. In small saucepan, melt butter. Add brown sugar and cream, stirring until smooth. Bring to boiling, stirring constantly; boil 1 minute. Remove from heat. Let cool to 110° on candy thermometer, or until bottom of saucepan feels lukewarm.

2. With electric mixer at medium speed, beat in powdered sugar until thick and smooth. Add vanilla. Spread on cool cake.

Patio Picnic

SPINACH-CHEESE PIE
Serves 8

1 9-inch pie shell, unbaked	1 8-ounce cup ricotta cheese
2 tablespoons butter	1 8-ounce cup cottage cheese
¼ cup chopped scallions	½ cup grated Parmesan cheese
1 10-ounce package frozen chopped spinach, thawed and well drained	¾ teaspoon salt
	Dash of nutmeg
	Dash of pepper
2 eggs, beaten slightly	

1. Preheat oven to 375°. Sauté scallions in hot butter. Add drained spinach to pan and stir minute or two. Remove from heat to cool.

2. Mix eggs with rest of ingredients. Stir in spinach mixture. Spoon into pie shell and bake for 45 minutes. Serve hot, cold, or at room temperature.

BARBECUED CHICKEN CHESTS
Serves 12

6 whole chicken breasts, split in two
1 lemon
¾ cup honey
1 cup catsup
¼ cup light corn syrup
2 tablespoons Worcestershire sauce

1. Lay chicken pieces in a large pan. Squeeze lemon juice over chicken. Combine rest of ingredients and pour over chicken. Marinate for at least one hour.

2. Grill chicken over hot coals, until done, or bake in oven at 350° for one hour and 15 minutes. (Baking chicken for 30 minutes in the oven before putting on grill cuts down grilling time.) Baste chicken once with honey mixture during baking.

BARBECUED SPARERIBS
Serves 4–5

Gail Brenner shared with me this method of cooking ribs. All the fat melts into the water in the broiler pan during baking, and the ribs remain moist and luscious. Since they are fully cooked before going on the grill, the barbecuing takes just a few minutes.

3 pounds baby back ribs
½ cup commercial barbecue sauce
¼ cup pancake syrup
3 tablespoons brown sugar

1. Two hours before serving, put ribs on top of broiler pan. Add water to broiler pan to depth of one inch. Cover ribs with foil. Bake at 350° for 1½ hours.

2. Mix barbecue sauce, syrup, and sugar together. Brush on ribs. Grill over hot coals about 5 minutes on each side or until sauce is bubbly and browned. Or, discard water and bake in 350° oven 30 minutes more, basting several times with sauce.

ALTERNATE SAUCE

½ cup pineapple juice   2 tablespoons soy sauce
½ cup dark corn syrup   1 teaspoon salt
½ cup apricot preserves   2 tablespoons brown sugar

Boil together 5 minutes and brush on ribs.

TIP: For a delicious garnish, brush fresh or canned pineapple slices with sauce and grill for several minutes. Serve on platter with ribs.

POTATO SALAD
Serves 6

4 medium large potatoes

Dressing

3 hard-cooked eggs (reserve 2 to   ¼ to ⅓ cup minced green pepper
   slice for garnish)   (optional)
½ cup mayonnaise   1 cup chopped celery
2 tablespoons fresh lemon juice   ½ teaspoon salt
½ cup yogurt or sour cream   ½ teaspoon dill weed or 2 tea-
½ cup minced green onions   spoons fresh dill chopped
½ cup sweet pickle relish   (optional)
3 tablespoons prepared mustard   ¼ teaspoon marjoram
1 garlic clove, minced   ½ teaspoon summer savory or
½ teaspoon Worcestershire   celery seed
   sauce   ⅛ teaspoon pepper
1 tablespoon minced parsley

1. In large saucepan, cook unpeeled potatoes until fork-tender, about 40 minutes. While potatoes are cooking, mix dressing. In medium bowl, mash egg thoroughly. Stir in all ingredients.

2. After potatoes are cooked, drain; plunge into cold water and drain immediately. Peel and cut into ½-inch cubes; pour dressing over warm potatoes and toss until well coated. Cool. Then cover and chill. Garnish with egg slices and parsley.

TOSSED SALAD
Serves 6

2 medium zucchini	1 green pepper
2 medium onions	1 carrot
3 peeled tomatoes	2 cucumbers, peeled
2 stalks celery	1 clove garlic, minced (optional)
1 cup broccoli or cauliflower flowerets	Italian salad dressing

Chop vegetables coarsely. Mix with garlic and small amount of dressing. Refrigerate. Serve alone or toss with lettuce. Keeps for several days in refrigerator.

MACAROON MARBLE CAKE
Serves 12

Filling

1 egg white (reserve yolk)	1 7-ounce package grated coconut
1 teaspoon vanilla	
½ cup sugar	1 tablespoon flour

Beat egg white with vanilla until soft mounds form. Gradually beat in sugar; then stir in coconut and flour. Set aside mixture.

Cake Batter

¼ cup cocoa	½ cup butter or Crisco
1 teaspoon instant-coffee powder	½ teaspoon salt
¾ cup hot water	2 teaspoons vanilla
3 eggs, separated	2 cups flour
½ cup sugar	1 teaspoon baking soda
1¼ cups sugar	½ cup sour cream

1. Preheat oven to 350°. Dissolve cocoa and coffee powder in hot water; cool. In bowl, beat 3 egg whites until soft mounds form; then beat in ½ cup sugar, until meringue stands in stiff peaks; set aside.

2. In large bowl, with mixer at medium speed, beat 1¼ cups

sugar, shortening, 4 egg yolks, salt, vanilla, and half of cocoa mixture until light. Stir in flour. Stir soda into sour cream, and add with rest of cocoa mixture; then fold in meringue.

3. Turn half of chocolate batter into 10-inch tube pan, greased on bottom only. Sprinkle with coconut mixture; then cover with rest of chocolate batter. Bake 1¼ hours or until top springs back when lightly touched with finger. Cool completely. Remove from pan; frost with Chocolate Glaze.

CHOCOLATE GLAZE

**1 6-ounce package of semisweet   1 tablespoon vegetable
   chocolate pieces   shortening
½ teaspoon vanilla extract**

In double boiler, over hot, not boiling water, melt chocolate pieces with vegetable shortening; add in vanilla extract.

Summer Serendipity

Sour Cream Quiche
Char-Broiled Beef Tenderloin
Asparagus Supreme Casserole
Molded Potato Salad
Watermelon Bowl
Lawn Fete Carrot Cake

SOUR CREAM QUICHE
Serves 6–8

1 9-inch pie shell, unbaked
2 medium onions, sliced
1 tablespoon oil
1 tablespoon butter
½ pound Swiss cheese shredded
1 cup milk
1 cup sour cream

3 eggs
½ teaspoon salt
1 tablespoon melted butter
Freshly ground pepper
Dash of nutmeg
2 drops Tabasco

1. Preheat oven to 350°. Sauté onions in hot oil and butter until tender. Sprinkle cheese in pie shell, then add onions on top.

2. Beat eggs; stir in milk, sour cream, salt, melted butter, pepper and nutmeg; pour into pie shell. Bake for 40 minutes or until puffed and golden.

CHAR-BROILED BEEF TENDERLOIN
Serves 20–24

3 whole filets of beef
Kitchen Bouquet

2 garlic cloves, cut in half
(optional)
Pepper

1. Rub Kitchen Bouquet over filets with your fingers. Brush or rub filets with garlic cloves. Sprinkle with pepper. Cut the thinner

half of filets off and set aside. Roast thick part in a 450° oven for about 20–25 minutes. Then grill both thin and thick parts over hot charcoal for 5 to 10 minutes on each side.

2. Slice into ½-inch pieces and arrange on a serving platter. You will have rare- to well-done slices. Garnish with sprigs of parsley. You may want to serve meat on lightly buttered French bread slices, arranged on platters.

ASPARAGUS SUPREME CASSEROLE
Serves 6

8 ounces sharp Cheddar cheese, grated
2 cups crushed Ritz crackers
¼ cup butter, melted
1 10¾-ounce can cream of mushroom soup

2 large cans asparagus spears, drained (reserve liquid)
½ cup almonds
1 2½-ounce can deviled ham (optional)

1. Combine cheese and crackers. Mix butter, soup, and reserved asparagus liquid together. Add ham if desired.

2. Layer in casserole in this order: cheese and cracker mixture, asparagus spears, almonds, half of soup mixture. Repeat process, ending with cracker mixture on top. Bake 30 to 40 minutes at 350°. This can bake longer. (Good for suppers that wait.)

MOLDED POTATO SALAD
Serves 12
Make it the day before. If not using mold, leave out gelatin mixture and serve salad heaped in a pretty bowl.

1½ envelopes unflavored gelatin
¼ cup cold water
1 cup hot water
¼ cup lemon juice
6 stuffed olives, sliced
3 hard-cooked eggs, sliced
1 teaspoon sugar
1 teaspoon salt
5 cups diced, cooked potatoes

¼ cup chopped green pepper
¼ cup chopped pimento
¼ cup chopped green onion
½ cup chopped celery
¼ cup snipped parsley
½ teaspoon salt
1½ cups mayonnaise
½ cup heavy cream, whipped

1. The day before serving, soften gelatin in cold water, then dissolve in hot water. Add lemon juice.

2. Pour small amount of gelatin mixture into 2-quart mold, or 2 smaller molds, swirling liquid until a thin layer coats sides and bottom. Arrange olive slices and egg slices in bottom of mold in decorative pattern. Put in refrigerator.

3. Allow rest of gelatin to thicken but not set. Prepare rest of ingredients; mix with thickened gelatin and spoon carefully into mold. Refrigerate overnight. Unmold on round serving platter. So pretty, it needs no extra garnish.

WATERMELON BOWL
Serves 24

1 large watermelon	1 pint blueberries
1 cantaloupe	1 fresh pineapple or can of pine-
1 pint strawberries	apple chunks
1 cup Florida orange sections	1 large bunch of green grapes

1. Early in the day, or day before, cut large slice off top of watermelon ⅓ of the way down. Set aside.

2. Scoop out watermelon with melon-ball scoop or measuring teaspoon. With drinking glass as guide, draw half-circles end to end, all around top of watermelon, making a scalloped design. Cut along scalloped design and trim edges so they look neat. Clean out inside of watermelon nicely, turn upside down on tray to drain, and refrigerate.

3. With melon scoop, make cantaloupe balls. Wash berries and grapes; drain on paper towels. Cut pineapple into chunks. Store fruits all together side by side in a large plastic-salad container, being careful not to mix them.

4. When ready to serve, mix together gently and heap into drained watermelon bowl. Use any fruits you like, but I think these look especially nice.

LAWN FETE CARROT CAKE
Serves 20–24

1 cup corn oil
2 cups sugar
4 eggs
2 cups flour
2 teaspoons cinnamon
2 teaspoons soda
2 teaspoons vanilla
2 teaspoons baking powder
½ teaspoon salt

Dash of allspice (optional)
1 apple grated (optional)
3 cups shredded carrots (about 5
    or 6 carrots) *or*
2 cups shredded carrots and 1
    cup shredded coconut
1 cup chopped walnuts or pecans
1 cup crushed pineapple includ-
    ing juice

Preheat oven to 350°. Combine all ingredients in large bowl. Pour into buttered and floured 10-inch tube cake pan or three 8-inch round cake pans and bake for 1 hour and 10 minutes. (Do not use a fluted tube pan). Either of the following frostings are terrific on this cake.

CREAM CHEESE FROSTING

1 16-ounce box powdered sugar
½ cup butter at room
    temperature

3 ounces cream cheese at room
    temperature
1 teaspoon vanilla

Blend until smooth. 1 teaspoon lemon juice or milk can be added if frosting is too thick. Decorate with nut halves.

BUTTERMILK GLAZE

⅔ cup sugar
⅓ cup buttermilk
2 tablespoons butter

1 tablespoon light corn syrup
¼ teaspoon baking soda
1 teaspoon vanilla

Combine all ingredients except vanilla in small saucepan and bring to boil over medium heat, stirring constantly. Reduce heat and simmer gently 5 minutes. Remove from heat and stir in vanilla. Pour over top of cake.

Light Fantastic

Grilled Shrimp with Spicy Barbecue Sauce
Sour Cream Deviled Eggs
Sauced Green Beans
Strawberries Devonshire
Kiss Cookies

GRILLED SHRIMP
Serves 8

40 medium or large shrimp, peeled, deveined, and well dried
16 medium or large mushrooms
1 onion, cut in 2-inch pieces

1 large green pepper, cut in 2-inch pieces
¼ fresh pineapple, cut in 2-inch pieces (optional)
1 box cherry tomatoes

SAUCE

½ cup olive oil
½ cup soy sauce
½ cup lime juice
2 shakes garlic salt or 1 clove garlic, minced

¼ cup chili sauce
Few grinds of black pepper
Dash of Tabasco

1. In 2-quart bowl, mix olive oil, soy sauce, chili sauce, lime juice, garlic salt, pepper, and Tabasco. Add shrimp and stir to coat well. Cover and refrigerate overnight, or at least several hours.

2. Drop onion and green pepper into boiling water for about ½ minute. Drain and dry thoroughly.

3. Skewer 5 shrimp, 2 onions, 2 mushrooms, 2 green peppers, 2 pineapple, and 2 tomatoes alternately on each skewer. Brush well with marinade. Place on barbecue and cook one side. Turn and cook second side until shrimp is pink and tender, just a few minutes on each side. Serve with Spicy Sauce if desired.

Spicy Barbecue Sauce
Makes 1 cup

1 cup catsup	1 tablespoon chopped chives or
¼ cup lemon juice	onions
6 drops Tabasco	Dash of salt

Mix all ingredients together. Serve at room temperature.

SOUR CREAM DEVILED EGGS
Serves 8

8 hard-cooked eggs, shelled	½ teaspoon lemon juice
2 tablespoons mayonnaise	¼ teaspoon dry mustard
2 tablespoons sour cream	¼ teaspoon salt
2 tablespoons minced onion	8 stuffed olives, halved (optional)

Cut eggs in half, lengthwise. Remove yolks to a small bowl and mash; add rest of ingredients except olives. Beat together until smooth. Spoon yolk mixture into each egg white. Top each with olive half. Chill several hours.

SAUCED GREEN BEANS
Serves 8

1 pound fresh green beans (or 3 10-ounce packages frozen green beans)	⅛ teaspoon thyme
	¼ teaspoon freshly ground pepper
5 tablespoons salad oil	1 teaspoon salt
2 tablespoons white vinegar	1 tablespoon Dijon mustard
¼ teaspoon coriander	1 small onion, halved
¼ teaspoon summer savory	½ cup mayonnaise

1. Wash and trim beans. Cook in boiling salted water, uncovered, for 8 to 10 minutes. Drain thoroughly. Cover, refrigerate.

2. Put all remaining ingredients in blender container. Blend until smooth. Cover and refrigerate. Pour dressing over beans when ready to serve.

STRAWBERRIES DEVONSHIRE

2 large oranges   1½ cups dairy sour cream
3 cups fresh strawberries   ½ cup firmly packed brown sugar

1. Strawberries are never ordinary, but to make them look even more special, slice 2 large oranges and place orange rounds on edge around inside of straight-sided, clear-glass serving bowl.

2. Wash and hull strawberries. Place in the serving bowl. Cover and chill.

3. Just before serving, mix sour cream and brown sugar in a small bowl. Beat until well combined. Serve with strawberries.

KISS COOKIES
Makes 4 dozen

1¾ cups unsifted flour   ½ cup creamy peanut butter
1 teaspoon baking soda   1 egg
½ teaspoon salt   2 tablespoons milk
½ cup sugar   1 teaspoon vanilla extract
½ cup packed light brown sugar   48 Hershey Chocolate Kisses
½ cup shortening

1. In large mixer bowl, stir flour, soda, and salt together. Add remaining ingredients except candy and mix at medium speed of electric mixer until well combined, scraping bowl occasionally. Chill dough 30 minutes.

2. Preheat oven to 375°. Roll small amounts of dough into 1-inch balls. Place on ungreased cookie sheet and bake for 12 minutes or until light brown. Remove from oven and immediately press chocolate kiss into center of each. (The cookie cracks around the edge.)

Private-Office Rendezvous (Dietetic!)

Pair White Boots or Heels
Trench Coat
Chilled Beverage in Thermos
Transistor Radio
Picnic Basket with Grapes (May or
may not be needed!)

13
The Boss Is Coming for Dinner

Can't Miss
Production Line
Promotion Time

The 10-Most-Asked Questions When the Boss Is Coming for Dinner

1. Why?
2. When?
3. Why not later?
4. Can't we eat out?
5. Don't you love me?
6. Is she (or he) coming, too?
7. What do they like?
8. What will she wear?
9. When will they leave?
10. Don't you love me?

Can't Miss

HOT CHEESE DIP
Serves 6

This is the favorite hors d'oeuvre of tennis pro Karol Fagaros Short, who shares it with us.

1 onion, chopped fine
2 tablespoons olive oil
2 tablespoons flour
2 6-ounce packages Monterey Jack cheese
1 10-ounce package Old English Sharp Cheddar cheese

1 10-ounce package Silver Kraft Mellow cheese
1 4-ounce can chopped green chilies (jalapeño peppers), or 5 green chilies, chopped
2 packages Dorito Chips

1. Brown onion in oil until transparent. Add flour to make paste.

2. Over low heat, add Monterey Jack, sharp Cheddar, and mild Cheddar cheese. Cover pan until cheese is melted.

3. Stir in chopped chilies. Transfer to buttered baking pan and refrigerate. Bake at 400° for 15 minutes and broil for 5 minutes before serving. Serve in chafing dish to keep it warm, with a bowl of Dorito chips alongside. The men will love this one.

STEAK DIANE
Serves 6

6 filet mignon steaks or 6 portions boneless sirloin steaks
Kitchen Bouquet (optional)
1 clove garlic, crushed
Salt and pepper to taste
1½ tablespoons olive oil
2 tablespoons butter
3 tablespoons chopped chives or
  shallots

½ teaspoon Dijon mustard
1 teaspoon Worcestershire
  sauce
2 tablespoons condensed beef
  broth or lemon juice
2 tablespoons chopped parsley

1. Flatten steaks slightly with side of cleaver to ¼- to ⅜-inch thickness. Rub each side of steak with crushed garlic and Kitchen Bouquet.

2. Melt butter with oil in skillet at a high heat. When butter is sizzling, add steaks. Cook about 2 minutes on each side. Remove to warm plate, and sprinkle steaks with salt and pepper.

3. Add chives or shallots to skillet; cook about 10 seconds. Stir mustard, Worcestershire sauce, and beef broth into skillet and heat to boiling. Return steaks to pan, spoon sauce over. Sprinkle with chopped parsley and freshly ground pepper, and serve on heated plates.

STUFFED MUSHROOMS
Serves 6

1 pound very large mushrooms
1 medium onion, chopped fine
⅓ cup butter
2 cups soft bread crumbs
1 tablespoon catsup or chili
  sauce
1½ teaspoons salt

¼ teaspoon pepper
1 tablespoon lemon juice
Few shakes of nutmeg (optional)
½ cup cream
½ cup finely chopped walnuts
  (optional)

1. Preheat oven to 400°. Wash and dry mushrooms. Remove stems and chop. Set caps aside. In melted butter, sauté chopped

stems with chopped onion and nutmeg. Add crumbs and cook 2 minutes. Stir in rest of seasonings and walnuts.

2. Stuff mushroom caps and arrange in glass baking dish. Pour cream over top. Bake 20 minutes.

SOUR CREAM POTATO CASSEROLE
Serves 8

6 medium potatoes, boiled
1 stick butter
1 pint sour cream
1 10¾-ounce can cream of mush-
    room soup
10 ounces Cheddar cheese,
    grated

½ cup grated onion
1 tablespoon Worcestershire
    sauce
Dash of cayenne pepper
    (optional)
2 tablespoons butter, melted
½ cup bread crumbs

1. Preheat oven to 350°. Peel and cut potatoes into small cubes.

2. Heat soup and butter in saucepan until both are melted; add sour cream.

3. Combine all ingredients in a large bowl. Spoon into 9 x 14-inch buttered casserole. Mix butter and crumbs and sprinkle on top of potatoes. (You may freeze casserole at this point.) Bake 45 minutes.

CAESAR SALAD
Serves 6

2 large heads of romaine lettuce
    (or part iceberg lettuce)
    washed and torn in large
    bite-size pieces
1 large egg at room temperature
4 tablespoons fresh lemon juice
4 anchovy fillets, drained and
    chopped fine
¼ teaspoon oil from anchovy can
2 teaspoons prepared mustard
    (optional)

⅓ cup olive oil
2 garlic cloves, minced
1 cup freshly grated Parmesan
    cheese
2 teaspoons Worcestershire
    sauce
Freshly grated pepper to taste
¾ cup croutons
Anchovy fillets for garnish
    (optional)

1. In large salad bowl mix garlic with anchovies to form a paste. Add anchovy oil. Beat egg in small bowl; add lemon juice, mustard, Worcestershire sauce, and oil. Mix well and add to anchovy mixture. Cover bowl and let dressing stand at room temperature.

2. At serving time, put lettuce in salad bowl and toss lightly with dressing. Add cheese, pepper, and croutons. Toss thoroughly. Pile on chilled salad plates. Arrange several anchovies on top of each salad, if you like.

COFFEE ICE-CREAM PIE WITH
HOT FUDGE SAUCE
Makes 2 pies, each serving 8
Having 1 or 2 of these pies in the freezer is great security.

1 15-ounce package Oreo cookies, crushed	**Dash of cinnamon (optional)**
½ cup butter, melted	**1½ quarts coffee (or other flavor) ice cream, softened**

Mix cookie crumbs with butter. Press into 2 buttered 9-inch pie pans. Bake for 5 minutes at 350°. Spoon ice cream into cooled pie shells and cover with plastic wrap and freeze.

TOPPING

⅔ cup sugar	**½ cup whipping cream**
⅓ cup water	**2 teaspoons cocoa**
2 egg whites	**⅛ teaspoon salt**

1. Combine sugar and water in saucepan. Boil 7 minutes until syrup spins a thread.

2. Meanwhile, beat egg whites until stiff. Add syrup slowly to egg whites, beating constantly, until meringue holds its shape. Chill.

3. In chilled bowl, whip cream, cocoa, and salt until stiff. Fold whipped-cream mixture into chilled meringue. Mound on pie. Return to freezer. Can be made up to 48 hours in advance. Twenty minutes before serving, take pie from freezer.

4. Make Fudge Sauce to drizzle over each piece of pie.

HOT FUDGE SAUCE

⅓ cup butter, softened   4 squares unsweetened
2½ cups powdered sugar   chocolate
⅔ cup evaporated milk   1 teaspoon vanilla

Mix all ingredients and cook over hot water for 30 minutes. Do not stir while cooking. Remove from heat and beat. Keep in refrigerator and reheat as needed. To thin sauce, add cream.

Production Line

Spinach Vegetable Dip
Baked Chicken en Crème
Savory Rice Pilaf
Sauced Asparagus
Fruit Salad with
Poppy Seed Dressing
English Toffee Squares

SPINACH VEGETABLE DIP
Serves 8

Every party should have one dish which involves dunking something into a dip. It allows for a dramatic pause in a conversation and it keeps a between-conversations guest busy. Here's a good one.

1 10-ounce package frozen, chopped spinach, thawed, drained, and squeezed
1 cup or a bit more sour cream
½ cup mayonnaise
1 envelope vegetable soup mix
1 8-ounce can water chestnuts, drained and chopped

¼ cup green onions or scallions, finely chopped
Dash of celery salt
Dash of lemon juice
¼ cup parsley, chopped (optional)

Mix all ingredients together and chill. Serve with vegetable strips or crackers. Makes 2 cups.

VEGETABLES FOR DIP

3 stalks celery
2 cucumbers
3 carrots
2 green peppers

2 yellow squash
2 zucchini
12 cherry tomatoes
1 clove garlic (optional)

1. Cut vegetables (except for tomatoes) into thin strips. Soak in bowl of water with ice cubes for 30 minutes.

2. Peel garlic clove and rub onto piece of waxed paper to coat paper. Wrap all drained vegetables in waxed paper, cover with dish towel, and keep in refrigerator until time to serve.

3. Just before serving, place Spinach Vegetable Dip in center of serving plate with vegetables surrounding it.

BAKED CHICKEN EN CRÈME
Serves 8

2 3-pound chickens, cut in pieces	**¾ teaspoon salt**
1 10½-ounce can cream of	**½ cup chopped onion**
chicken or mushroom soup,	**1 clove garlic, minced**
undiluted	**1 4-ounce can chopped**
½ cup apple cider	**mushrooms**
2 tablespoons Worcestershire	**Paprika**
sauce	

1. Early in day, put chicken pieces in 13 x 9 x 2-inch pan. Blend all ingredients except paprika and pour over chicken. Sprinkle generously with paprika. Refrigerate.

2. Bake 2 hours or until tender, basting with sauce occasionally.

SAVORY RICE PILAF

¼ cup slivered almonds	**¼ teaspoon thyme**
¾ cup chopped onion	**¼ teaspoon sage**
1 cup chopped celery	**Dash of pepper**
¼ cup butter, divided	**2½ cups water (boiling)**
1 cup rice	
1 package dry chicken-noodle	
soup mix	

1. Sauté almonds in two tablespoons butter until lightly browned. Remove almonds with slotted spoon; set aside. Add rest of

butter to skillet. When foamy, add onions, celery, and rice and sauté until golden, stirring occasionally.

2. Transfer rice mixture to saucepan. Stir in rest of ingredients and bring to boil. Cover with tight lid and turn heat to simmer. Simmer ½ hour. Do not lift lid.

SAUCED ASPARAGUS
Serves 8

3 10½-ounce cans asparagus
    tips, well drained
1 cup sour cream

¼ cup mayonnaise
½ cup grated Parmesan cheese
¼ cup grated Cheddar cheese

Arrange asparagus in broiler-proof dish. Combine remaining ingredients and spread over asparagus. Broil until lightly browned and bubbly. Serve immediately.

FRUIT SALAD
Serves 6

2 oranges, peeled and cut in
    sections
1 apple (or any fruit such as
    pears, peaches, or cherries)
1 cup strawberries, cut in half
½ cup green grapes

1 banana, sliced and dipped in
    orange or lemon juice
2 cups watermelon or canta-
    loupe balls or a combination
    of both
Romaine lettuce leaves

Mix all fruits except banana and chill. Just before serving, gently mix in sliced banana. Line serving bowl with romaine leaves, and heap fruit on top. Serve with POPPY-SEED DRESSING on the side.

VARIATION: For a lovely exotic touch add avocado balls made from two avocado halves. If you have an abundance of avocados, serve individual salads piled in avocado halves. To prepare halves, peel and brush lightly with lemon juice inside and out.

POPPY-SEED DRESSING
Makes 3 cups

1½ cups sugar
2 teaspoons dry mustard
2 teaspoons salt
⅔ cup vinegar or fresh lemon juice

2 tablespoons finely grated onion
2 cups salad oil (not olive oil)
3 tablespoons poppy seeds
Few drops red food coloring (optional)

Combine sugar, mustard, salt, vinegar, and onion in container of electric blender or food processor. Add oil very slowly, beating constantly until thick. Stir in poppy seeds and food coloring. Store covered in cool place or refrigerator. If mixture becomes too hot or too cold, it will separate.

ENGLISH TOFFEE SQUARES
Serves 8–10

4 tablespoons melted butter
1½ cups vanilla wafers, crushed
1½ cups chopped nuts
2 cups powdered sugar
1 cup butter
6 egg yolks

3 squares unsweetened chocolate, melted
1 teaspoon vanilla
6 egg whites, beaten until stiff
1 cup heavy cream, whipped (optional)

1. Mix butter, wafer crumbs, and nuts together and press half of mixture on bottom of 8 x 12-inch pan. Set aside.

2. Cream powdered sugar and 1 cup butter. Add 6 beaten egg yolks, melted chocolate, and vanilla. Fold in stiffly beaten egg whites. Pour over crumb mixture in pan. Sprinkle remaining crumbs on top. Chill overnight.

3. To serve, cut in squares and top each with a dollop of whipped cream, if desired.

VARIATION: Half the wafer mixture can be pressed into 12 cupcake papers set in muffin tins. Spoon cream mixture into papers. Sprinkle remaining crumbs on top. Freeze.

Promotion Time

DEVILED CRAB
Serves 6

1 pound fresh or frozen crab
    meat
¼ cup butter
1 cup chopped celery
1 onion, chopped
1 teaspoon thyme
½ teaspoon salt
½ teaspoon pepper
¼ cup mayonnaise
1 teaspoon lemon juice

1 egg, beaten
1 tablespoon Worcestershire
    sauce
1 teaspoon dry mustard
3 drops hot pepper sauce
1 tablespoon chopped parsley
Dash of cayenne pepper
2 cups soft bread crumbs,
    divided
2 tablespoons melted butter

1. Break crab up in small pieces and remove any bits of shell.

2. In melted butter, sauté celery and onion with thyme, salt, and pepper. Add crab meat, and cook 1 minute.

3. Mix together mayonnaise, lemon juice, egg, 2 sauces, dry mustard, parsley, cayenne pepper, and 1 cup bread crumbs. Stir into crabmeat mixture. Spoon into 6 buttered crab shells or individual baking dishes (ramekins).

4. Toss remaining 1 cup bread crumbs with 2 tablespoons

melted butter and sprinkle over each portion. Bake at 375° until brown, about 15 minutes. Serve with lemon wedges, if desired.

ROAST BEEF TENDERLOIN
Makes 8–10 servings

1 6-pound whole beef tenderloin	Kitchen Bouquet
1 clove garlic	Freshly ground pepper

1. About 1¼ hours before serving, preheat oven to 450°. Remove any surface fat and connective tissue from tenderloin. Rub surface with garlic and Kitchen Bouquet. Press fresh pepper in meat.

2. Place on wire rack in shallow open pan, tucking narrow end under to make roast more uniformly thick. Insert meat thermometer into center at thickest part. Roast about 60 minutes or until thermometer reads 140°. Meat is crusty brown outside, pink to red inside.

3. Cut tenderloin into 1-inch thick slices; arrange on heated platter. Spoon BÉARNAISE SAUCE over slices or serve it from gravy boat.

BÉARNAISE SAUCE

3 shallots or little green onions, chopped fine	½ cup butter, softened
1 teaspoon dried tarragon	½ teaspoon salt
¼ cup wine vinegar	Dash of Tabasco
¼ cup white vinegar	2 teaspoons chopped parsley
1 tablespoon lemon juice	3 egg yolks

1. Bring to boil in saucepan shallots, tarragon, and both vinegars. Boil until sauce becomes glaze.

2. In heavy saucepan, mix egg yolks and lemon juice with wire whisk. Over *low* heat or hot water, beat in butter, 1 tablespoon at a time, until thickened. Stir in glaze and rest of ingredients. Serve warm with roast beef.

TIP: If your children are artistically inclined, enlist their help in making onion chrysanthemum.

ONION CHRYSANTHEMUM
To garnish platter of large roast.

1. Peel medium, uniformly shaped onion; cut thin slice from top. Cut crosswise into quarters to within ½ inch of bottom. After all wedges are cut, force toothpicks into bottom of each cut.

2. To color, place onion upside down in water deeply colored with red, orange or yellow food coloring. Let stand at room temperature 24 hours.

3. Drain "flower" thoroughly; remove toothpicks; lightly press petals outward. Or use a purple onion, but omit food coloring. Chill in iced water to spread petals.

POTATOES ANNA
Serves 4–6

½ cup soft butter
5 or 6 large all-purpose potatoes, peeled (Do not let potatoes stand in water; they need their starch for this recipe.)

1 to 2 teaspoons salt
½ teaspoon freshly ground black pepper
¼ teaspoon freshly grated nutmeg (optional)

1. Preheat oven to 425° about 1½ hours before serving. Melt 3 tablespoons butter in 8-inch ovenproof skillet equipped with tight-fitting cover or covered with foil.

2. Slice peeled potatoes into ⅛-inch thick slices to make about 4 cups. Pat very dry on paper towel. Gently toss potatoes with salt, pepper, and nutmeg. Layer a third of potato slices, circular fashion, overlapping around bottom and sides of skillet. Drizzle with one tablespoon melted butter. Repeat, overlapping in opposite direction. Drizzle with one tablespoon butter. Repeat process, using up all of potatoes. Cover with buttered double thickness of foil and press

down on potatoes with heavy pan. Cook this way over direct, medium-high heat for 15 minutes. Remove foil and pan.

3. Move skillet to oven and bake, uncovered, 30 minutes or until tender. (Place sheet of foil under skillet to catch any runover.) Remove skillet; with lid on top of potatoes, carefully pour off excess butter. Remove lid. Potatoes can be kept warm for up to 30 minutes. To serve, loosen by running knife around edge of skillet, invert on serving platter. Cut in wedges to serve.

VAR'ATION: Add one onion, thinly sliced between 2 layers of overlapping potatoes.

ZUCCHINI AND CARROTS JULIENNE
Serves 6

2 tablespoons butter
2 tablespoons oil
6 medium zucchini, cut into
    julienne strips

6 medium carrots, cut into
    julienne strips
Salt and freshly ground pepper

Heat butter and oil in large skillet or wok over high heat. Add vegetables and stir-fry until tender but crisp. Sprinkle with salt and pepper, and serve hot.

TOMATO AND CUCUMBER SALAD WITH
VINAIGRETTE DRESSING
Serves 6

3 ripe tomatoes, sliced
3 cucumbers, sliced
1 red or purple onion, sliced
¼ cup wine vinegar
3 tablespoons Dijon mustard
1 teaspoon dried tarragon

1 teaspoon salt
1 teaspoon dry mustard
½ teaspoon sugar
¼ teaspoon freshly ground
    pepper
¾ cup olive oil

1. Arrange tomato, cucumber, and onion slices in shallow serving dish. Mix rest of ingredients in blender. Pour over vegetables just to cover. Chill thoroughly.

2. To serve, arrange vegetables on individual salad plates lined with lettuce leaves. Spoon dressing on top.

STRAWBERRY CHEESECAKE SUPREME
Serves 14

CRUST

1¼ cups sifted flour	1 egg yolk
¼ cup sugar	½ cup butter, room temperature
1 tablespoon grated lemon peel	½ teaspoon vanilla

FILLING

5 8-ounce packages cream cheese, room temperature	1½ teaspoons grated lemon peel
	1 teaspoon vanilla
1¾ cups sugar	5 eggs
3 tablespoons flour	2 egg yolks
1½ teaspoons grated orange peel	¼ cup whipping cream

1. Preheat oven to 400°. Combine flour, sugar, and lemon peel. Make a well in center and drop in egg yolk, butter, and vanilla. Quickly work together until well blended. Wrap in waxed paper and chill 1 hour.

2. Roll out ⅓ of dough to ⅛-inch thickness. Fit over bottom of buttered 9-inch springform pan. Trim and save extra dough. Bake circle of dough about 8 minutes or until golden brown. Cool.

3. Butter sides of pan and place sides over bottom of pan. Turn oven up to 500°. Roll out remaining dough and line pan ¾ of the way up sides. Set aside.

4. Blend together cheese, sugar, flour, just until smooth. Add eggs and yolks one at a time, mixing well after each addition. Blend in rest of ingredients. Pour into springform pan and bake 12 minutes. Reduce heat to 275° and bake 45 minutes. Turn off oven. Let cheesecake remain in oven 30 minutes. Remove. Cool in a draft-free place.

5. Several hours before serving, make strawberry glaze:

STRAWBERRY GLAZE

1 quart fresh strawberries, washed and hulled	Pinch of salt 1 teaspoon butter
¾ cup sugar	Few drops red food coloring
¼ cup cold water	(optional)
1½ tablespoons cornstarch	

1. Reserve largest and most attractive berries for top of cheese-cake. Crush about 1 cup berries in saucepan; add sugar, water, cornstarch, and salt. Stirring constantly, boil mixture for about 2 minutes. Blend in butter.

2. Remove from heat, pour into blender and puree. Let cool slightly. Remove sides of cheesecake pan. Arrange whole berries on cheesecake and spoon glaze over all. Chill several hours.

VARIATION:

CRUMB CRUST

¾ cups graham-cracker crumbs	2 tablespoons butter, melted
1½ tablespoons sugar	2 tablespoons chopped walnuts
¼ teaspoon cinnamon	

1. Generously grease 9 x 3-inch springform pan with butter. Place pan in center of a 12-inch circle of aluminum foil and press foil up around side of pan.

2. Combine graham-cracker crumbs, sugar, cinnamon, melted butter, and nuts in small bowl until well blended. Press crumb mixture into bottom and side of pan. Chill prepared pan while making filling.

3. Proceed with instructions as outlined above.

14
Rainy-Day Projects

Grease
Long, Cold Winter
Long, Hot Summer
Mother's Contribution

The Day the Kids Took Over the Kitchen

What made that particular Saturday so special? Michelle, age seven at the time, had wandered into the kitchen. She observed me for a few moments and suddenly announced, "Mom, I want to cook something, too."

I had previously told her, "Look, anytime you kids want to cook, just let me know, and I'll even clean up the mess." I was so generous with my services because I wanted my girls to grow up capable of creating their own masterpieces for the eye to behold and the palate to savor. And besides, why couldn't they be trained to help, and ease my work load (my real reason)? I was willing to help them learn, and now Michelle was taking me up on my offer.

"Just think, Mom," she said, "this is what you've always dreamed of."

"You're absolutely right," I beamed.

She said, "I want to invent my own recipe." She refused my advice to follow a surefire recipe and was determined to bake a "cake" according to her formula.

"Mom," she said, "I'll write down just what I'm putting in, so you can make it later if you want." The top of her paper read "Bake Reciept."

Michelle went to the refrigerator and took out a carton of sour cream, two eggs, and milk from the bottom shelf. The thought crossed my mind, *Eggs are too expensive to waste,* but I quickly rejected that objection, realizing that Michelle's few ingredients were much less costly than a cheap toy, and would probably keep her occupied far longer.

"First, you put in a little bit of each of these," she explained, sounding like a pint-sized Julia Childs, as she dropped in a large glob of sour cream, a cup of milk, and eggs, complete with some of the shell for "crunchiness."

Next came an uncertain quantity of flour, sugar, chocolate chips, a small box of raisins, and quite a bit of vanilla.

The telephone rang, so, while I was gone for five minutes, a few other secret ingredients were added to the potion.

Michelle then folded the mixture into a big glob, laid it on a cookie tray, and slid it into the hot oven. "Call me when it's ready, Mom," she said with great pride, and off she went.

I was rather curious about this recipe. I wasn't quite sure whether it would rise or congeal or explode. But while it was brewing, I remembered my dream of children in the kitchen. I even smiled as I began to wipe down the cupboards and floor and walls.

Michelle came by regularly to check her "cake," standing on a chair to peek into the oven. She finally declared "OK, Mom, that's enough. It's ready now. Let's try it."

I carefully removed the "substance" and tried to cut it into little wedges. Michelle took one look and bent over to smell it. Then she wrinkled her nose and said, "Mom, *you* better try it."

She wouldn't touch it. No one would touch it, much less taste it. So I bravely ate it, or, rather, chewed it briefly, solely as a tribute to Michelle's first cake.

I know I'll never forget the taste, nor will I forget Michelle's wide-eyed, one-tooth-missing grin as she watched me with great pleasure. And neither of us will ever forget the memory of that day—the oneness we experienced during that second Saturday in March.

Grease

QUICK TOMATO SOUP
Serves 6

2 10½-ounce cans condensed tomato bisque soup, undiluted
2 10½-ounce cans of chicken
broth
½ teaspoon freshly grated
pepper
2 tablespoons light brown sugar

1 tablespoon Worcestershire
sauce
2 tablespoons lemon juice
Dash of cloves
Dash of marjoram (optional)
Lemon slices (optional)

Mix soup, chicken broth, pepper, brown sugar, and Worcestershire sauce in saucepan. Simmer for 5 minutes. Add lemon juice,
cloves, and marjoram; serve in mugs. Garnish with lemon slices, if
desired.

FRENCH-TOASTED TUNA SANDWICHES
Serves 4

7-ounce can tuna, drained and
flaked
2 tablespoons well-drained
sweet-pickle relish
1 tablespoon chopped onion
(optional)
½ cup finely chopped celery
⅓ cup mayonnaise

½ cup grated Cheddar cheese
(optional)
8 slices bread
2 tablespoons butter
2 eggs
3 tablespoons milk
Dash of salt
Dash of pepper

1. Combine tuna, relish, onion, celery, and mayonnaise. Spread tuna filling on 4 slices of bread. Top with remaining slices.

2. Heat butter in large heavy skillet. Beat eggs, milk, salt, and pepper together. Pour into pie plate or shallow dish. Dip sandwiches quickly into egg mixture to coat both sides. Brown slowly in skillet.

FRENCH-TOASTED HAM SANDWICHES
Serves 4

8 slices cooked ham
8 slices white bread
3 slightly beaten eggs
1 tablespoon water
1½ cups (6 ounces) shredded
    Swiss cheese

½ cup milk
½ cup mayonnaise or salad
    dressing
Dash of ground nutmeg (op-
    tional)

1. Place 2 slices of ham on four bread slices; top with second slice bread. Halve each sandwich diagonally. In shallow dish beat eggs and water until combined; dip sandwiches into egg mixture.

2. Grill on griddle or in lightly greased skillet over medium heat about 2 to 3 minutes on each side. Place 2 of sandwich halves in each of 4 individual, shallow casseroles. Set aside.

3. In small saucepan combine cheese, milk, and mayonnaise. Stir over low heat until cheese melts and mixture thickens. Pour over toasted halves. Sprinkle with nutmeg. Broil 4 to 5 inches from heat until just bubbly, about 3 minutes.

YOU-CAN-EAT-IT DOUGH

1¼ cups powdered sugar   1 cup corn syrup
1¼ cups powdered milk   1 cup peanut butter

Mix all ingredients well until dough reaches proper consistency for modeling. Let children sculpt "fantabulous" creations, then let them *eat* the arty creations once they've been admired!

ICE-CREAM MUFFINS

1 cup self-rising flour   1 cup vanilla ice cream

Preheat oven to 350°. Mix together and turn into greased muffin tins, or tins lined with cup cake papers, so muffin pans stay clean. Bake for 12 minutes.

Long, Cold Winter

TOE-WARMER APPLE JUICE
Serves 6

1 46-ounce can apple juice
¼ cup brown sugar
½ cup orange juice

1-inch cinnamon stick
6 whole cloves

Mix all ingredients together in saucepan. Bring to boil, turn down heat and simmer 15 minutes. Strain before serving.

PIGGIES IN A BLANKET
Makes 8

8 hot dogs
1 package refrigerated crescent
dinner rolls
Prepared mustard

2 egg yolks, lightly beaten
1 tablespoon water
1 tablespoon caraway seeds
(optional)

Preheat oven to 375°. Unroll dough, separating into 8 triangles. Spread each piece of dough lightly with mustard. Place hot dogs at wide end of triangles and roll up. Brush dough with egg yolks beaten with 1 tablespoon water. Sprinkle with caraway seeds and press lightly into rolls. Bake on cookie sheet 15 minutes or until golden. Serve hot with relishes.

HOT CINNAMON MOCHA
Serves 8

1 6-ounce package (1 cup) semi-
    sweet chocolate pieces
1¼ cups strong coffee (in place
    of brewed coffee, use 1 tea-
    spoon instant coffee mixed
    with 1¼ cups boiling water)

2 teaspoons ground cinnamon
Dash of salt
6 cups milk
2 tablespoons sugar (optional)
½ teaspoon vanilla

1. Heat and stir chocolate, coffee, cinnamon, and salt over medium-low heat until chocolate is melted and mixture is smooth. Stir in milk, sugar, and vanilla.

2. Beat chocolate mixture with rotary egg beater till foamy. Pour drink into mugs.

PEANUT BUTTER FUDGE

1 cup granulated sugar
1 cup brown sugar
½ cup evaporated milk
Dash of salt
1 cup marshmallow cream

¾ cup smooth or crunchy peanut
    butter
1 tablespoon butter
1 teaspoon vanilla

1. Stir sugars, milk, and salt together in sauce pan. Bring to boiling, and boil 5 minutes, stirring constantly.

2. Stir in marshmallow cream, peanut butter, butter, and vanilla. Pour into 9 x 9-inch square buttered pan. Cool, and cut in squares.

BRAN BREAD

3½ cups unsifted flour
½ cup instant nonfat dry milk
1½ teaspoons salt
2 packages dry yeast
¼ cup sugar
1½ cups warm water (105° to
    115°)

2 cups All-Bran or Bran Buds
    cereal
⅓ cup softened butter
1 egg (room temperature)

1. In large bowl, stir together 3 cups flour, nonfat dry milk, and salt. Set aside.

2. Combine yeast, sugar, and warm water in another large bowl. Stir in All-Bran cereal. Let stand about 2 minutes or until cereal is softened. Add butter, egg, and about half of flour mixture. Beat at medium speed 2 minutes, scraping bowl occasionally.

3. Stir in remaining flour mixture by hand. Add ½ cup flour, if necessary, to form stiff, sticky dough. Cover; let rise in warm place, free from draft, until double in bulk, about 1 hour.

4. Stir down dough. Place into 9 x 5 x 3-inch buttered loaf pan. Bake in preheated oven 375° about 40 minutes or until done. Remove from pan. Brush top of loaf with melted butter if desired. Cool on wire rack.

GINGERBREAD BOYS
Recipe makes a lot of boys!

1 cup shortening
1 cup light brown sugar
1 cup molasses
2 tablespoons distilled white
    vinegar
1 large egg
5 cups flour

½ teaspoon salt
1½ teaspoons baking soda
2 teaspoons ground ginger
1 teaspoon ground cloves
1 teaspoon cinnamon
½ teaspoon nutmeg
1 teaspoon vanilla

1. Cream shortening and brown sugar together. Beat in eggs. Stir in molasses and vinegar.

2. Sift dry ingredients together. Add ⅓ at a time to egg mixture, beating until smooth. (You may have to use your hands.)

3. Chill dough for at least 3 hours. Cut off piece of dough and refrigerate rest until ready for it. Toss on floured tea towel or pastry cloth. Roll to ⅛-inch thickness; cut with cookie cutters dipped first into flour before cutting.

4. Place cookies on lightly greased cookie sheet and bake in preheated 350° oven for 8 to 10 minutes, until edges brown. Remove to racks to cool before frosting.

ICING PAINT

1½ cups sifted powdered sugar   **Dash of salt**
2 egg whites   **1 teaspoon vanilla**

Beat ingredients at high speed. Put in small bowls and add coloring to each. Cover bowl with damp cloth until ready for use. Apply with a brush.

NOTE: If not planning to frost cookies, sprinkle with sugar or decorative toppings. (I freeze half the dough for another "cookie" day.)

OATMEAL ICEBOX COOKIES
Makes 80

1 cup flour   **⅛ teaspoon ground cloves**
⅓ cup nonfat dry milk   **1 cup butter, softened**
¼ cup toasted wheat germ   **½ cup brown sugar, packed**
¼ cup unprocessed bran   **2 eggs**
    (optional)   **1 teaspoon vanilla**
1 teaspoon baking soda   **1 teaspoon lemon juice**
½ teaspoon salt   **3½ cups rolled oats (not instant)**
1 teaspoon cinnamon   **1 cup chopped walnuts**
¼ teaspoon nutmeg

1. Stir together flour, dry milk, wheat germ, bran, soda, salt, and spices. Set aside.

2. In large bowl of mixer, cream butter and sugar. Add eggs, lemon juice, and vanilla; beat until fluffy. Gradually stir in flour mixture just to blend. Stir in oats and walnuts until well blended.

3. Divide dough in half. Shape dough into rolls about 1½ inches in diameter. Wrap in waxed paper and chill in refrigerator overnight, or in freezer for 2 hours.

4. With serrated knife, slice rolls into ¼-inch-thick slices; place 2 inches apart on foil-lined cookie sheets. Bake in preheated 350° oven 10 to 12 minutes or until browned. Slide foil with cookies off cookie sheet, cool slightly. Remove cookies to racks to cool completely. Store in airtight container.

Long, Hot Summer

JIFFY PIZZA SNACKS
Serves 4

2 English muffins, split, buttered, and toasted
1 8-ounce can pizza sauce (or catsup)

1 small hunk salami or pepperoni, or 2 hot dogs sliced thin
½ cup grated mozzarella cheese

Spoon several spoons of pizza sauce on each muffin, covering evenly. (If no pizza sauce or catsup on hand, use 1 8-ounce can tomato sauce, mixed with ¼ teaspoon pepper, ¼ teaspoon sweet basil, ¼ teaspoon oregano, and ¼ teaspoon salt.) Arrange salami, pepperoni or hot dog slices over sauce. Sprinkle evenly with cheese. Broil for a few minutes, until cheese melts.

GRANDMA'S BANANA BREAD

2 cups all-purpose or whole wheat flour
1 teaspoon baking soda
1 teaspoon cream of tartar
½ teaspoon salt
½ cup lightly salted butter, at room temperature
¾ cup white or light brown sugar
2 large eggs

1 cup walnuts or pecans, chopped
½ teaspoon grated lemon rind (optional)
1½ cups mashed ripe bananas (about 3 medium bananas)
2 tablespoons hot water
1 teaspoon vanilla
Apricot Glaze (optional)

1. Preheat oven to 350°. Grease 9 x 5 x 3-inch loaf pan. Mix flour with baking soda.

2. In large bowl, beat butter and sugar until smooth and creamy. Add eggs, one at a time, beating well after each addition. Stir in pecans, lemon rind, and mashed banana.

3. Add flour mixture, ½ cup at a time, beating well after each addition. Stir in water and vanilla and pour into prepared pan.

4. Bake 55 to 60 minutes, or until cake tester inserted in center of bread comes out clean. Remove bread from pan and put on wire cake rack. Cool completely. Serve with cream cheese. Makes 1 loaf, about 10 servings.

NOTE: For best flavor use very ripe bananas, those with speckled-leopard skins. I prefer to use 3 smaller bread pans rather than the standard 9 x 5-inch loaf pan. Smaller loaves (3½ x 7½ x 2-inch) pans are perfect for my family. You can freeze the extra loaves or send one to your neighbors.

QUICK APRICOT GLAZE

½ cup apricot preserves   1 teaspoon sugar

Heat preserves and sugar in pan until ingredients bubble. Strain mixture and brush evenly on cooled bread.

GRAPE DROPS

2 cups seedless green grapes

Freeze grapes on cookie sheet. Serve as snack straight from freezer. Store in plastic bag in freezer. Sweet and nutritious.

LEMONADE-STAND BROWNIES
Makes 24

⅔ cup all-purpose or whole-   ¾ cup brown sugar, packed
   wheat flour   2 eggs

½ teaspoon baking powder
¼ teaspoon salt
½ cup crunchy peanut butter
¼ cup butter at room
temperature

2 teaspoons vanilla
3 squares semisweet chocolate
or ½ cup semisweet choco-
late pieces, melted and
cooled

1. Mix flour, baking powder, and salt; set aside.

2. In small bowl cream peanut butter, butter, and brown sugar until light. Add eggs and vanilla; beat until fluffy. Stir in flour mixture just to blend.

3. Spread in greased 8-inch square baking pan. Drizzle on chocolate, then with table knife swirl into batter to marbleize. Bake in preheated 350° oven 25 to 30 minutes or until pick inserted in center comes out clean. Cool in pan on rack. Cut into 24 bars.

Mother's Contribution

Meat Sauce Base for:
Spaghetti
Sloppy Joes
Chili
Hamburger Supreme

While the kids are creating concoctions, you might as well be stirring up a sauce that will feed the masses in the days to come. Here is a meat sauce that can be used for four different dishes—Spaghetti, Sloppy Joes, Chili, and Hamburger Supreme.

MEAT SAUCE BASE

3 pounds ground beef	2 8-ounce cans tomato sauce
2 or 3 green peppers, chopped	½ teaspoon oregano
2 or 3 onions, chopped	1½ teaspoons salt
2 cloves garlic, minced (optional)	¼ teaspoon ground pepper
2 1-pound 12-ounce cans tomatoes	1 teaspoon sugar

1. Brown beef in large skillet; remove meat to large cooking pot.

2. In skillet, cook onions and peppers until soft; transfer to meat in pot. Add rest of ingredients and bring to boiling; lower heat and simmer one hour.

Divide sauce into four portions (about 3 cups sauce in each).

1. For SPAGHETTI: Add to 1 portion, one 15½-ounce jar commercial spaghetti sauce. Freeze. Prepare an 8-ounce package of spaghetti to serve 4 to 6.

2. For SLOPPY JOES: Add to 1 portion, 1 10½-ounce can chicken gumbo soup, undiluted, 1 packet Sloppy Joe seasoning mix or ½ cup commercial barbecue sauce, and one tablespoon prepared

mustard. Simmer until heated through. Freeze. Reheat and spoon over split, buttered, toasted hamburger buns to serve 6 to 8.

3. For CHILI: Add to 1 portion, 1 can kidney beans, ¼ teaspoon paprika, ½ teaspoon sugar, ½ to 1 teaspoon chili powder and dash of crushed red pepper (optional). Freeze. Simmer until heated thoroughly. Serves 4.

4. For HAMBURGER SUPREME: Add to 1 portion, 3 tablespoons dry onion-soup mix. Cook noodles according to directions on package; drain. Mix together ½ cup cottage cheese and 5 ounces mozzarella cheese, grated. To assemble, cover bottom of 8 x 12-inch baking dish with ⅓ of meat sauce, add half of noodles, half of cheese mixture, ⅓ of meat sauce; repeat layer. Sprinkle 3 tablespoons Parmesan cheese on top (optional). Bake at 350° for 25 minutes. Serves 6.

15
Stand Up and Cheer

Giving Thanks (A Holiday Buffet)
Special Friends
Happiness Is. . . .
Happy Birthday to the King

Gift Sampler

"Mom! Get up!" I heard my eight-year-old bundle of energy (also known as Michelle) exclaim. "It's only six more shopping days 'til Christmas!"

I pulled the covers back over my head, but then the second wave hit me as Laura pounced on the bed with that unnerving news, "Quick, Mom, get up! You've got to take us to the mall. C'mon! We're all ready. Let's go!"

Panic invaded my sleepy soul. My heart began to pound, as all the projects of the day came crashing into my consciousness.

I chased them out of the room and then whispered a prayer. "Lord, Help! Here I am; I'm coming first to You. I don't want to panic. I don't want to run in circles. I am not a creature of fate, but a woman of ordained destiny. Please take this day and go before me. Make the crooked places straight as You promised. Arrange my day according to Your will—the cleaning, the meals, the presents. Help me remember that *You* are my satisfaction. I can't even breathe unless You permit it."

Suddenly my world became meaningful. The work was still there, but the panic was gone. Instead of my projects controlling and overpowering me, *I* was in control. No, better yet, the One who set the boundaries of the seas and the orbits of the planets—*He* was in control.

As I flew into action, I breathed another prayer: *Happy birthday, Lord! And when this holiday is over, please don't let me lose the meaning of it all.*

My girls caught the difference. On the way home from shopping later that day, Michelle said, "Mommy, when you have Jesus in your heart, *every* day is Christmas."

My mind returned to Christmas in Ohio. The year was 1945. I was just a little girl, waiting for my daddy outside the front door of the cluttered hardware store on our city square.

Inside the heated building, my coat, scarf and leggings had nearly smothered me, as I stood first on one leg and then another, dripping melting snow from my boots into an ever-expanding puddle on the clean, wooden floor. I still remember the angry voice of the shopkeeper sending me outside.

The sky was already turning dark, and I began to think about dinner. I watched the hordes of giant people, hurrying in and out of stores with bundles sticking out from under their arms. On the corner stood the Salvation Army man in a Santa suit, methodically ringing his bell, as coins periodically clanked into his kettle. Christmas carols floated through the cold air, "The hopes and fears of all the years are met in Thee tonight."

I was aware of all the Christmas hustle, but down inside this little girl, there was a deeper awareness. I looked up past the street lights and watched dazzling snowflakes, swirling into view out of the darkness, and felt them landing lightly on my face.

As I stood against the building and watched the crowds push by, suddenly I felt an intense longing, a desperate longing for home—not the house in which I lived, but my *real* home. I couldn't understand just what I was feeling.

The snow fell relentlessly from the dark and endless sky. Questions swirled like snowflakes in my mind: *What is beyond the sky? Is my real home up there? What is Christmas all about? Why do I feel sad and homesick?*

The exquisite beauty of the scene enveloped my senses—the cold wind carrying the joyful songs, the wet snow on my lips, the snowflake diamonds, dancing before my eyes across the shafts of light, yet—deep within—a heart that ached and didn't know why.

Just then my daddy hurried out of the hardware store, and we trudged our way home. But the Lord of Christmas had pulled at my heart. God had placed the ache there to gain my attention. And He got it.

When I was twenty-three, I finally realized that the significance of Christmas was Messiah's birthday—God, come to earth, born as a Hebrew baby, just as the Prophet Isaiah proclaimed He would. When I trusted that God of Abraham, Isaac, and Jacob as *my* Messiah, He took away the ache. Beautifully, powerfully, peacefully.

Today as a grown woman, that same Lord continues to fill me with joy. Of course, life is still a struggle; problems, at times, seem overwhelming. But there is *more,* much more. Like joy. And love. And abundant life. Jesus Himself said, "In the world you have tribulation, but be of good cheer, for I have overcome the world."

Someday we can check into a new abode, a veritable mansion, with no more sorrow. God Himself will wipe away all our tears.

Even death will die. Talk about good news! These words are true. There *is* a new world coming, and one day soon the Lord will return as King!

I'd like to shout it from the rooftops, "We have hope! The real purpose of life is available. Accept your free sample today (it's really that easy!). The Greatest News that ever could come to man's ears has come! So, stand up and cheer!"

Giving Thanks (A Holiday Buffet)

Holiday Punch
Roast Turkey with Herb Stuffing
and Gravy
Creamed Mashed Potatoes
Baked Fruit Compote or
Holiday Frozen Fruit Salad
Broccoli with Cheese Sauce
Pecan Pie

HOLIDAY PUNCH
Makes 34 servings, ½ cup each

1 46-ounce can of Hawaiian Punch, chilled

1 46-ounce can of pineapple juice, chilled

1 12-ounce can of frozen orange juice, undiluted

4 cups sparkling cider or ginger ale, chilled

Combine all ingredients in large punch bowl. Float orange slices or strawberries on top. For a more festive touch, scoops of raspberry sherbert may be added.

ROAST TURKEY
Serves 20–24

1 12 to 14 pound turkey   ½ cup butter, melted

1. Remove giblets from fresh or thawed turkey; cover with water in small saucepan and simmer giblets and neck to make stock for dressing or gravy.

2. Rinse turkey thoroughly with cold water; pat dry with towel. Sprinkle inside cavity with regular or seasoned salt. Add Herb Stuffing. Tie ends of legs to tail with cord or string. Lift wingtips up and over back, so they are tucked under bird.

3. Brush entire bird with melted butter; place breast side up on rack in roasting pan. Insert meat thermometer in breast or fleshy part of thigh next to body not touching bone.

4. Roast uncovered at 325° until thermometer registers 190°, about 4 hours. When turkey turns golden brown, cover lightly with aluminum foil.

5. After about 4 hours, cut cord holding legs to tail, so insides of thighs will be fully cooked. Turkey is done when drumsticks move up and down easily. Wait 20 minutes before carving.

HERB STUFFING
Makes about 6 cups, enough for 12-pound turkey.

⅔ cup butter	¼ cup chopped parsley
1½ cups celery, finely chopped	¼ teaspoon thyme
1½ cups onions, finely chopped	¼ teaspoon salt
1 8-ounce package herb-seasoned stuffing mix	¼ teaspoon pepper
	1¼ cups chicken broth, heated

1. In large saucepan or Dutch oven, melt ⅓ cup butter and add chopped celery and onions. Sauté over medium-low heat until tender.

2. Add remaining ⅓ cup butter to pan and increase heat to medium. Stir in stuffing mix and seasonings. Pour in hot broth and toss lightly with fork until mixture is moistened. Stuff into cavity of turkey.

GRAVY
Makes 2 cups

4 tablespoons fat from roasting pan	2 cups broth from giblets (or half milk, half broth)
4 tablespoons flour	Salt and pepper to taste

In skillet over medium heat, add flour to hot fat, stirring until nicely browned. With whisk, stir in liquid; bring to boiling point and simmer. Add salt and pepper and simmer a few minutes longer.

CREAMED MASHED POTATOES
Serves 6

3 to 4 pounds all-purpose pota-   ½ to 1 cup hot milk or cream
toes, peeled and cut into   1 egg yolk (optional)
halves   1 teaspoon salt
6 tablespoons soft butter, cut   ½ teaspoon pepper
into 6 pieces

1. Place potatoes in saucepan and cover with water and 2 tea-spoons salt. Partially cover and boil over moderate heat 30 to 35 minutes, until potatoes are tender.

2. Drain potatoes in colander; then put through food mill or ricer placed over saucepan they were boiled in. (If you don't have food mill or ricer, push potatoes through metal strainer with back of wooden spoon; use masher as last resort.)

3. Place pan over moderate heat and shake for 2 minutes to dry out potatoes. Beat in butter, 2 or 3 pieces at a time, and salt and pepper. Add hot cream slowly, beating to consistency you prefer. Beat in egg yolk and salt and pepper. Mashed potatoes can be kept hot or reheated in top of double boiler over simmering water.

BAKED FRUIT COMPOTE
Serves 6–8
Delicious hot or cold, as accompaniment with meat or poultry. Also delicious as topping over ice cream.

2 cinnamon sticks   Shredded peel of one lemon
6 cloves   (optional)
1 package pitted prunes   1 can cherry pie filling
1 package dried apricots or   ½ cup red grape juice
peaches   ½ cup pineapple juice
1 can pineapple chunks, drained   3 tablespoons sugar
(save juice)   ¼ teaspoon cinnamon
1 cup fresh orange sections, or 1
11-ounce can mandarin or-
anges (drained)

1. Preheat oven to 325°. Stew prunes and apricots until soft in water with cinnamon sticks and cloves. Drain.

2. Arrange fruit in deep baking dish in layers, first prunes, then apricots, pineapple, oranges, lemon peel, with cherry filling on top.

3. Mix grape and pineapple juice with sugar and cinnamon. Pour over top. Bake 1 hour. Transfer to chafing dish for special effect.

HOLIDAY FROZEN FRUIT SALAD
Serves 10

1 quart vanilla ice cream or ice milk

½ cup sour cream

1 8¼-ounce can crushed pineapple, drained

1 10-ounce pack frozen raspberries, partially thawed

1 16-ounce can whole-berry cranberry sauce

½ cup chopped pecans

½ cup green grapes, halved and seeded (optional)

Lettuce leaves

Line muffin pans with 10 cupcake papers, or use a 9 x 5 x 3-inch loaf pan. Stir ice cream and sour cream together. Fold in rest of ingredients. Spoon mixture into cupcake papers or loaf pan. Freeze until firm. To serve, place individual serving on lettuce leaf on salad plate.

BROCCOLI WITH CHEESE SAUCE
Serves 6–8

2 bunches broccoli, cooked and drained

1 11-ounce can condensed Cheddar cheese soup

½ cup sour cream

1 cup grated Swiss cheese

1 teaspoon lemon rind

1 tablespoon lemon juice

Arrange cooked broccoli in serving dish. Keep warm. Mix rest of ingredients in saucepan and stir over medium heat until cheese melts. Pour over cooked broccoli and serve.

PECAN PIE
Serves 8

3 eggs, slightly beaten
1 cup dark corn syrup (I often
   use ½ cup dark and ½ cup
   light corn syrup)
¼ teaspoon salt

2 teaspoons vanilla
¾ cup sugar
2 tablespoons butter, melted
2 cups pecans, halves or chopped
1 9-inch unbaked pastry shell

1. Mix all ingredients for filling together, adding pecans last.
2. Pour into pastry shell. Bake in preheated 400° oven 15 minutes; reduce heat to 350° and bake 30 to 35 minutes longer. Outer edges of filling should be set, center slightly soft. Cool at room temperature. Serve with ice cream if desired.

VARIATION: HONEY PECAN PIE.   Substitute 1 cup honey for 1 cup corn syrup.

Special Friends

SPICED HOT CIDER PUNCH
Makes 24 servings, ½ cup each

1½ cups sugar
½ cup water
12 whole cloves
3 pieces candied ginger or
    dash of powdered ginger
    (optional)

2 2-inch pieces cinnamon stick
6 cups grapefruit juice
3 cups orange juice
1 quart cider

1. In saucepan, combine sugar, ½ cup water, cloves, cinnamon, and ginger; bring to boiling. Reduce heat, and simmer 20 minutes. Strain.

2. In large bowl, combine fruit juices and cider; mix well. Stir in sugar syrup.

3. Reheat, and serve hot. If desired, garnish with orange slices and cinnamon sticks. (Punch is also very good chilled. May be made up to 2 weeks ahead, and reheated over and over, as needed.)

JALAPEÑO CHEESE WEDGES
Serves 6

3 slices cooked bacon, crumbled
5 green onions with tops, thinly
   sliced
4 eggs
½ cup half-and-half
1 4-ounce can chopped green
   chilies (jalapeño peppers)

¼ teaspoon salt
Dash of hot pepper sauce
⅛ teaspoon ground pepper
2 cups shredded Monterey Jack
   cheese or Cheddar cheese
1 teaspoon melted butter

1. Preheat oven to 300°. Sauté onions in 1 tablespoon bacon fat over low heat until transparent, about 5 minutes.

2. Whisk eggs in medium-size bowl, until blended; stir in all ingredients except butter. Pour mixture into buttered 10-inch pie plate or a 9-inch square baking dish. Drizzle top with melted butter. Bake at 300° until set and light brown on top, 35 to 40 minutes. Cut into wedges. Serve hot.

BEEF STROGANOFF
Serves 4

½ pound fresh mushrooms,
   sliced
½ cup finely chopped onion
3 tablespoons butter
2 pounds filet of beef, cut into
   thin, bite-size strips
1 teaspoon salt
¼ teaspoon paprika
½ teaspoon Kitchen Bouquet
   (optional)
1 garlic clove, minced

2 tablespoons catsup
1 10½-ounce can condensed beef
   bouillon, undiluted
3 tablespoons flour
½ cup sour cream (more if
   desired)
1 tablespoon Worcestershire
   sauce
8-ounce package of noodles,
   cooked according to directions on package

1. Early in the day, or the day before, melt butter in skillet; add mushrooms and onions. Sauté until golden. (Butter foams when heated. When foam subsides, butter is at right temperature for

sautéing). With slotted spoon, remove mixture from skillet and set aside.

2. In same skillet, brown beef strips quickly, in several batches, being careful not to overcrowd meat as it browns. Add salt, paprika, Kitchen Bouquet (if desired), garlic, catsup, and bouillon. Simmer 10 minutes.

3. Pour off ½ cup liquid into small bowl. With wire whisk or spoon, stir flour into liquid to make smooth paste. Then stir paste into meat mixture. Add onions and mushrooms, and continue to heat and stir until thickened. Refrigerate until dinnertime.

4. Just before serving, reheat mixture; add sour cream and Worcestershire sauce and heat through. Serve on bed of noodles. Add ½ teaspoon caraway seed for exotic touch.

FRENCH PEAS
Serves 6

2 packages frozen peas, cooked and drained	6 green onions, chopped
	½ teaspoon nutmeg
6 tablespoons butter	2 tablespoons cream or milk

Cook butter, onions, nutmeg, and cream in skillet until bubbly. Add peas. Heat through.

ASPARAGUS, TOMATO, AND MUSHROOM SALAD
Serves 4

1 bunch of fresh asparagus (about 16 stalks)	½ teaspoon sugar
	2 large tomatoes, peeled and sliced thinly
½ pound mushrooms, wiped clean with damp cloth and cut into thin slices	1 large ripe avocado, cut in thin slices (optional)
½ teaspoon salt	Juice of 2 lemons

1. Sprinkle mushroom and avocado slices with lemon juice. After discarding the white area and running cold water over each stalk to remove grit, lay asparagus on bottom of skillet and cover

with ½ inch of boiling water. Add ½ teaspoon salt and ½ teaspoon sugar. Boil uncovered 1 to 4 minutes depending on thickness of stalks. Remove from heat and let stand 6 minutes. Drain and chill.

2. Arrange on 4 salad plates, fanning the avocado, mushroom, and tomato slices out attractively. Lay asparagus on top of vegetables. Spoon dressing generously over salad.

VINAIGRETTE DRESSING

7 tablespoons salad or French peanut oil
1½ tablespoons wine vinegar
1 tablespoon Dijon mustard

Salt and pepper to taste
1 tablespoon finely chopped shallots or green onions (optional)

Beat all ingredients together with whisk or fork until well mixed. Refrigerate any leftover dressing.

STRAWBERRY GLACÉ PIE
Serves 8

9-inch baked pie shell, cooled

¼ cup finely chopped almonds (optional)

GLACÉ

1 cup sliced strawberries
½ cup sugar
Dash of salt

2 tablespoons cornstarch
1 tablespoon lemon juice
Few drops red food color

FILLING

3 cups strawberries
1 8-ounce package cream cheese,
at room temperature
2 tablespoons sugar

1 teaspoon grated orange peel
2 tablespoons orange juice, cream, or milk
¼ teaspoon almond extract

1. Make glacé: In medium saucepan, crush berries with potato masher or fork. Add ½ cup sugar, salt, and ¼ cup water.

2. Over medium heat, stirring constantly, bring to boiling. Cook 3 minutes; remove from heat. Mix cornstarch with ¼ cup water. Stir into berry mixture. Cook 2 minutes more until thick. Strain, if desired. Add food color and lemon juice. Set aside to cool.

3. Proceed with filling. Gently wash remaining berries in cold water. Drain; hull; dry.

4. In medium bowl, with portable electric mixer, beat cheese, sugar, orange peel and juice, cream or milk, and extract until light and fluffy. Sprinkle almonds in bottom of pie shell, if desired, and spread cream filling over baked, cooled pie shell.

5. Arrange strawberries, stem end down, evenly over cream-cheese mixture. Pour cooled glacé over berries. Refrigerate until chilled, about 3 hours. Serve with whipped cream.

VARIATION #1: In place of strawberry glacé (above), use Apricot Glaze. Combine 1 12-ounce jar apricot preserves, a few drops of red food coloring, if desired, and 2 tablespoons water. Boil until it reaches a thin consistency. Strain and spoon over berries.

VARIATION #2: Mix 1 cup sugar and 2 tablespoons cornstarch in saucepan. Add 1 cup water, and cook, stirring until thick and clear. Remove from heat and stir in 1½ tablespoons strawberry Jell-O mix. Cool; spoon over strawberries in pie shell.

Happiness Is. . . .

CREAM OF ONION SOUP
Serves 6–8

1 stick butter
2 pounds onions thinly sliced
   (7 cups)
2 teaspoons salt
¾ cup flour
2 10½-ounce cans beef stock

2 10½-ounce cans chicken stock
2 cups whipping cream or half-
   and-half
4 egg yolks beaten
Dash of nutmeg

CROUTONS

8 slices of French bread, ½- to
   1-inch thickness
2 teaspoons olive oil
1 garlic clove, cut

1 cup grated, imported Swiss
   cheese
1 cup freshly grated Parmesan
   cheese

1. In skillet melt butter over moderate heat. Stir in onions and salt and cook uncovered over low heat, stirring occasionally. Onions will turn rich golden brown. Sprinkle flour over onions and cook, stirring for three minutes. Stir stock and cream into onions slowly. Simmer for another 40 minutes. If too thick add more liquid. Taste for seasoning and add salt and pepper if needed. Add 4 beaten egg yolks to a small amount of hot soup. Then stir into rest of soup in skillet. Heat but do not boil. Add dash of nutmeg.

2. While soup simmers, make croutons. Preheat oven to 325°. Spread slices of bread in one layer on baking sheet and bake for 15 minutes. With pastry brush, lightly coat both sides of each slice with

olive oil. Then turn slices over and bake for another 15 minutes or until bread is completely dry and lightly brown. Rub each slice with cut garlic clove and set aside.

    3. Fill individual bowls with soup, add croutons, and sprinkle lots of cheese on top. Put lid on until cheese is melted, or place in oven until cheese has melted.

STUFFED CABBAGE WITH FLANKEN
Serves 8–10

1 teaspoon citric acid or sour salt	1 cup raisins (I like to use golden ones)
¼ cup water	1 1-pound jar sauerkraut, undrained
2 pounds ground beef	
¼ cup uncooked rice	1 cup dark brown sugar
1 large onion, chopped	1 teaspoon citric acid (optional)
1 carrot, grated	2 pounds German-style flanken without bone
1 teaspoon salt	
¼ teaspoon pepper	3 soupbones (optional)
1 large cabbage	2 bay leaves
2 6-ounce cans tomato paste	18 gingersnap cookies
1 2-pound can tomatoes	

    1. Preheat oven to 325°. Mix citric acid in water. Add ground beef, rice, onion, carrot, salt, and pepper. Mix thoroughly. Set aside.

    2. Heat large pan of water to boiling. Core cabbage and place cored side down in boiling water. Simmer for about six minutes. Remove from water and peel off 12 leaves. (You may want to scrape heavy vein in each leaf to make it lie flat.) Put portion of meat mixture (about ¼ cup or less) in each leaf. Roll up leaf, tucking in ends. Set aside.

    3. In large saucepan, combine tomato paste, tomatoes, raisins, sauerkraut, sugar, citric acid, soupbones and 9 crumbled gingersnaps. Stir and cook over low heat for 1 hour, stirring occasionally. Remove bones.

    4. In large oven-proof pot spread 1 cup of sauce. Arrange flanken on top of sauce. Place cabbage rolls, seam side down on top of

flanken. Pour rest of sauce over top. Cover tightly with foil and place on baking pan to catch drippings. Bake for 2½ hours.

5. Remove from oven; add bay leaves and rest of crumbled gingersnaps. Stir them gently into sauce on top. Continue baking uncovered for 30 minutes more. Remove bay leaves.

6. To serve, arrange cabbage rolls at one end of large platter, flanken at the other; pour sauce over all. This is even more luscious the following day. Freezes well too.

POTATO PANCAKES
Makes 12

4 large potatoes (2 pounds) pared and placed in ice water	¾ teaspoon salt
	Dash each of nutmeg and pepper
¼ cup grated onion	Salad oil, shortening, or
2 eggs, slightly beaten	chicken fat, for frying
2 tablespoons flour or matzo meal	Chilled applesauce or sour cream
Pinch of baking soda	

1. Just before using, grate potatoes on medium grate. (Potatoes turn dark if grated too far ahead.) Drain very well; pat dry with dish towel; measure 3 cups.

2. In large bowl, combine grated potato with onion, eggs, flour, salt, nutmeg, and pepper.

3. In large, heavy skillet, slowly heat oil, ⅛-inch deep, until very hot but not smoking.

4. For each pancake, drop potato mixture, 2 tablespoons at a time, into hot fat. With spatula, flatten against bottom of skillet to make a pancake 4 inches in diameter. Fry 2 or 3 minutes on each side, or until golden-brown. Drain well on paper towels. Serve hot with applesauce or sour cream.

GREEN BEANS WITH PARSLEY BUTTER
Serves 10–12

3 9-ounce packages frozen
   green beans
¼ cup butter
1 tablespoon chopped parsley
1 teaspoon freshly grated lemon
   peel

1 tablespoon fresh lemon juice
Dash of white pepper
Dash of marjoram or basil
   (optional)
1 cup finely chopped salted peanuts (optional)

Prepare beans according to directions on package. Drain beans and add rest of ingredients. Mix lightly and serve.

RASPBERRY BOMBE WITH STRAWBERRY SAUCE

1 quart vanilla ice cream, slightly
   softened
½ cup chopped nuts

½ cup chopped maraschino
   cherries
1 quart raspberry sherbert

1. Fold nuts and cherries into vanilla ice cream. Set 1 cup of mixture in freezer, and spread rest of mixture on sides and bottom of 2-quart mold, leaving center hollow. Freeze until firm.

2. Spoon sherbert into ice-cream-lined mold. Smooth reserved 1 cup of ice-cream mixture over top. Cover tightly with plastic wrap. Freeze until firm, about 4 hours.

3. Dip frozen mold in hot water 30 seconds, unmold on serving plate. Serve with Strawberry Sauce.

STRAWBERRY SAUCE
Makes 1⅓ cups

1 10-ounce package frozen sliced
   strawberries, thawed
¼ cup sugar

1 tablespoon cornstarch
2 tablespoons strawberry
   preserves

1. Drain berries; reserve syrup. Add water to syrup to measure 1 cup. In small saucepan, combine sugar and cornstarch. Gradually

add strawberry syrup, stirring until smooth. Over low heat, slowly bring to boiling, stirring until mixture is thickened and translucent.

2. Remove from heat. Stir in berries and preserves. Stir until melted. Refrigerate until cold.

CHOCOLATE FUDGE
Makes 2¼ pounds

1½ cups sugar
1½ cups light brown sugar
¾ cup butter
⅔ cup undiluted evaporated milk
1 7-ounce jar marshmallow
    cream

2 cups (12-ounces) semisweet
    chocolate pieces
2 teaspoons vanilla
1½ cups chopped nuts

1. Mix in heavy 2-quart saucepan the sugar, butter, evaporated milk, and marshmallow cream. Bring to bubbling boil quickly, stirring constantly. Reduce to medium heat when bubbles appear all over top; stir and cook 8 minutes.

2. Remove from heat and add semisweet chocolate pieces. Stir until completely melted and blended into mixture. Add vanilla and chopped nuts. Pour into greased 8- or 9-inch square pan. Cool thoroughly. Cut into squares as desired.

Happy Birthday to the King

Spinach Balls
Swiss Cheese Puffs
Standing Rib Roast
Browned Potatoes
Baked Carrots
Yorkshire Pudding
Bibb Lettuce with Dijon Dressing
Coffee-Toffee Pie

SPINACH BALLS
Makes 70
These delicious appetizers are perfect with any meal.

2 boxes frozen spinach, cooked, chopped, and well drained
2 cups Pepperidge Farm Herb Seasoned Stuffing Mix
6 eggs, beaten
2 large onions, chopped fine
¾ cup margarine, melted
½ to ¾ cup grated Parmesan cheese
¾ tablespoon garlic powder
½ tablespoon thyme
1 teaspoon black pepper
½ cup chopped parsley (optional)

Mix well, form in small balls. Place on cookie sheet; freeze. Place in plastic bags in freezer until needed. Bake frozen in pre-heated 375° oven, 20 minutes.

SWISS CHEESE PUFFS
Makes 30

½ cup mayonnaise
¼ cup chopped onion
2 tablespoons chopped parsley
2 cups grated Swiss cheese
30 tiny rye-bread slices
⅛ teaspoon cayenne pepper

Toast bread slices. Mix rest of ingredients together and spread on bread slices. Broil 2 to 3 minutes, or until puffed and golden.

STANDING RIB ROAST AND BROWNED POTATOES
Serves 8

3-rib standing rib roast (about 8 pounds)
2 teaspoons Kitchen Bouquet (optional)
1 garlic clove, cut in two
1½ tablespoons soft butter
Freshly ground pepper
8 potatoes, peeled
⅓ cup butter, melted
Parsley sprigs

1. Preheat oven to 425°. Rub cut-garlic halves over roast; discard garlic. With fingers, rub Kitchen Bouquet over roast. Smear soft butter over cut ends and sprinkle with pepper. Place meat, rib-side down, on rack in open pan. Stick meat thermometer in center of roast.

2. Roast meat 15 minutes at 425°. Then reduce heat to 325°, and roast until thermometer registers rare at 140°, allowing about 20 minutes per pound. One hour before roast is done, arrange potatoes around roast. Pour melted butter over them and sprinkle with salt and pepper. Twice during the remaining roasting time, turn potatoes so they will brown evenly, and baste them and meat with pan juices.

3. When meat is done, remove from oven, cover with foil, keep in warm place (near oven); wait 20 minutes before carving. Serve on platter surrounded by potatoes and garnished with parsley sprigs.

BAKED CARROTS
Serves 4

1 pound whole carrots
¼ cup mayonnaise
2 teaspoons minced onion
1 teaspoon prepared horseradish
Salt and pepper to taste
3 tablespoons finely crushed Ritz crackers
1 tablespoon butter
Parsley, chopped

1. Preheat oven to 375°. Cook carrots in boiling, salted water until tender. Save ¼ cup of cooking liquid. Cut carrots lengthwise in narrow strips. Place in 9-inch square baking dish; set aside.

2. Mix ¼ cup cooking liquid with mayonnaise, onion, horse-radish, salt and pepper. Pour over carrots and sprinkle crumbs on top. Dot with butter and sprinkle with parsley. Bake for 20 minutes.

YORKSHIRE PUDDING
Serves 6

I remember my mother serving Yorkshire Pudding on Thanks-giving and I loved it, even as a child. I was especially surprised by the taste, since I thought all puddings should be sweet. This dish is the hit of any party!

⅞ cup sifted flour	2 eggs
½ teaspoon salt	¼ cup hot roast drippings or
½ cup milk	melted butter
½ cup water	

1. Mix flour, salt, milk, and water. Beat eggs and stir into mixture. Beat well. Cover and refrigerate for one hour. One hour before dinner, take batter out of refrigerator and let it come to room temperature.
2. Preheat oven to 400°. Put drippings or butter in 12 x 7-inch or 13 x 9-inch baking dish and heat in oven. Beat batter again briefly and pour into hot baking dish.
3. Bake 20 minutes at 400°. Reduce heat to 350° and bake 15 minutes more. Cut in squares and serve immediately.

BIBB LETTUCE WITH DIJON DRESSING
Serves 4

4 small bunches Bibb lettuce	1 tablespoon Dijon mustard
8 cherry tomatoes, cut in half	2 green onions, chopped
2 tablespoons tarragon or wine vinegar	Pepper to taste
	½ cup olive oil
1 teaspoon salt	

Arrange Bibb lettuce in salad bowls, opening leaves to look like a rose. Top with tomato halves and onions. Mix rest of ingredients except oil. Add olive oil slowly while beating. Drizzle evenly on top of salads.

COFFEE-TOFFEE PIE
Makes 2 pies, each serving 8
Make one for tomorrow and one for the freezer. Takes time and love; but worth it when you hear the compliments. Spectacular!

CRUST

2 cups flour
¾ cup butter at room
  temperature
½ cup light brown sugar
1½ cups walnuts, finely chopped

2 squares baking chocolate,
  grated
1 tablespoon vanilla
1 tablespoon water if necessary

1. Preheat oven to 375°. The day before serving, mix flour, sugar, walnuts, and chocolate together. Add butter and vanilla and cut in with pastry cutter or two knives until mixture is crumbly. Add water if mixture is too dry.

2. Press into two 9-inch well-buttered pie pans. Prick crusts all over. Bake 15 to 20 minutes, or until lightly browned. Cool on wire rack.

MOCHA CREAM FILLING

½ cup butter, softened
1½ cups white or light brown
  sugar
1½ tablespoons instant coffee
  powder

4 eggs
2 squares unsweetened chocolate, melted and cooled
1 teaspoon vanilla

1. Combine all ingredients and beat with electric mixer at low speed for 10 minutes.

2. Pour into completely cooled pie shells, cover with wax paper and refrigerate. If you are going to freeze one pie, this is the time to do it. Pie to be used should be refrigerated overnight before topping is added.

TOPPING

3 cups heavy cream
1 tablespoon instant coffee
    powder
½ cup powdered sugar

1½ cups sliced almonds
    (optional)
1 square semisweet baking
    chocolate, grated coarsely
    or shaved

1. Next day, combine the heavy cream, instant coffee, and sugar in a large bowl, and refrigerate several hours.

2. At least 2 hours before serving, whip coffee-cream mixture until stiff. Spread thickly over both pies with a broad knife, covering filling and crust. Mound cream high in center. Sprinkle with sliced almonds and shaved chocolate. Refrigerate one until serving time, and return other to freezer. *Grand and glorious!*

No cookbook ever ends. This one will keep changing and growing as long as food and I are both on the same planet.

I have enjoyed sharing my favorites with you. If you have some special recipes of your own, I'd love to hear from you. Please write me at Post Office Box 380277, Miami, Florida 33138.

Wishing you total joy,

Marabel Morgan

Index